INTUITION

FOR

EVERY DAY

Book 3 "Living your Higher Self" Series

Second Edition

Enhancing Intuition
Master Workbook

Charol Messenger

INTUITION FOR EVERY DAY

Book 3 "Living your Higher Self" Series
Enhancing Intuition Master Workbook

Second Edition

Copyright © 2012-2018 by Charol Messenger

ISBN-13: **978-1-7320717-3-5**
Library of Congress Control Number: 2011914491

February 28, 2018 SECOND EDITION includes new Bowker ISBN, National Finalist Book Award and *many* reviews; new cover, book description, and author bio. Plus condensed to original manuscript to reduce the page volume. Original materials © 1975-2018.

Messenger Publishing
The New Humanity Author
Denver, Colorado   thenewhumanityauthor.com
charolmessenger.com   CharolM@aol.com

CreateSpace.com/**8191657**   Plus IngramSpark and more.

New cover art: "Yin Yang Human" by Bruce Rolff, ID 157255388, Shutterstock, standard license.

Reviews

practices for developing intuition along with Charol's real-life examples. Her stories are something the average person can relate to and be willing to try. I did and was amazed at the results! There is something to learn in every chapter. Whether you are experienced in metaphysical modalities or just learning, you will find this workbook to be the perfect guide on your path."

Judith Yarrow-Lawn, holistic health teacher

"I appreciate Charol's down-to-earth, practical spirituality way of assisting one in finding the answers from within, listening to details that one often ignores, and trusting one's deeper intuition to find solutions to the many challenges one is confronted with daily.... I have known Charol over many years and have read a number of her works, taken classes from her and appreciated the wisdom she imparts. Charol is guided by her inner wisdom and a strong sense of purpose to heal the planet. This book empowers you for your own personal healing journey."

"Charol Messenger's workbook *Intuition for Every Day* and her book *The Soul Path* have helped me to grow intuitively and I am able to use her techniques in everyday life. They also have helped me to become more grounded and relaxed. I recommend her books to anyone who wants to get rid of stress and realize their greater potential in life."
~ Danielle, age 18, Denver

"Clairvoyant Charol Messenger has written a brilliant collection of life's lessons—divinely inspired methods for finding our inner self. *Intuition for Every Day* energizes and soothes all at the same time. As Charol teaches how we can awaken our inner light and incorporate our divine essence in our daily life, the real meaning of our existence emerges. An unbelievable textbook of knowledge ... unprecedented in metaphysical circles ... step-by-step directions to integrate the Higher Self into everyday life." ~ Noel Brock, author of *The Lady in Blue,* and Director of Ancillary Services in a Georgia hospital

USA BEST BOOKS
National Finalist in New Age Nonfiction 2015

In a deep meditation, my oversoul spoke into my heart-mind and said, "My name is Samuel."

I saw him in a dream one quiet afternoon in Colorado during a short nap.

I looked up and this very handsome man in his forties walked toward me, dressed in a modest, brown monk's robe with a hood.

He came to me like a father. He came to me as a friend. He came without grandeur, but with a clear and steady gentleness.

And I knew: This is one called Oversoul. This one is the source of my being. This one is the purpose of my life, and I am to teach his message, given to each of us on Earth:

"Be who you are, now, today. And fear not. For the true divinity, the wisdom, the strength, the guidance, is not an outer force or magic—but is you yourself.

"*You* are the one who creates your life, your reality, your joy, your sorrow. *You* are the one with the power to change it.

"The Divine Light is in all, without exception. You find that light when you pause in your busy life—and allow the breath of life to carry you into the womb of creation ... where you were born and always will exist.

"You and all around you are a part of one Living Consciousness. And it is good. And so are you."

Enhancing Intuition
Master Workbook

Intuition for Every Day is a clairvoyant's Master Workbook of 43 years, with 130 original techniques, meditations, and visualizations to show you:

- How to *know* when you're in danger and how to protect yourself.

- How to *inner hear* (clairaudience) and how to know it isn't your own thoughts.

- How to *inner see* (clairvoyance) and the meanings of inner-vision symbols and metaphors.

- How to *sense/feel* (clairsentience) when something or someone is trouble or can be trusted.

Beginner to advanced meditations and techniques include: how to still the mind's chatter, block other people's thoughts and energy, meditate in motion, transmute the body's cellular structure into a light body, and integrate Higher Self consciousness (*knowing*).

A Higher Self activated clairvoyant, empath, channel of higher consciousness, and urban shaman (instinctively recalled from past lives), Charol Messenger also shares 29 personal anecdotes on how all of these methods have helped her; including protection from catastrophic weather (tornado, flash flood, forest fire, hurricane), as well as safeguarding and finding her lost dog.

My eternal love for my mom DJ who always believed in me. I dedicate all of these books to her, gentle and sweet spirit.

Also my love to my sister Jo, for our friendship.

My eternal gratitude to my dearest friend Barbara Munson for her irreplaceable support and friendship. She keeps me motivated and encouraged, and she is always there for me when I need another pair of eyes on final details.

My deep gratitude to Keith Klein and Mary Ann Klein. Their limitless grace allows me to do this fulfilling work with contentment.

My great appreciation to the thousands who have participated in the teachings given in these books; especially the *many* good souls who have gifted me throughout my life in innumerable ways, including: John Brennan, Marja Pheasant, JoAnn Goldsmith, Matthew Patterson, John Cloonan, and Ray Alcott.

Especially, I owe everything to the divine beings who guide me: my oversoul and soul council, the Angels of Serendipity, and the All Mind from whom all wisdom flows.

The Author

Futurist and global visionary Charol Messenger activated into Higher Self consciousness during a spontaneous awakening to cosmic consciousness and oversoul merge in 1975.[1]

Her books have received thirteen awards, including First Place Winner *The New Humans* (Book 2 *"The New Humanity"* series) in the Soul-Bridge Book Awards of Europe 2017 in the category "Spiritual Awakening of Humanity," as well as Second Place International Book Excellence Award 2017 (sole Finalist) in Spirituality; plus three more Book Excellence Awards in 2016 include: First Place Winner *You 2.0* in Personal Growth, and Second Place Winner *Humanity 2.0* (Book 1 in *"The New Humanity"* series, fourth award) (sole Finalist) in Spirituality.

A *spiritual revealer* attuned to the undercurrent hum sweeping through humanity, Charol has helped over 65,000 individuals through her Higher Self books, blogs, classes, tweets and 20,500 spiritual soul readings as a Higher Self clairvoyant.

A certified lightworker (1990), certified clear channel of Ascended Masters and the Spiritual Hierarchy (1983), and messenger of her oversoul and Angels of Serendipity, in the Messenger books Charol is revealing Higher teachings on spiritual development, the new millennial spirituality, Higher Self integration for everyday life, understanding the inner voice, communicating with the angels, and humanity's spiritual transcendence and long-foretold evolutionary transformation—that is happening *right now*. Humanity is in *transcension*. We are in it, now.

Founder of the Books for Iraq charity and international newsletter *Global Citizen*, Charol has a B.A. in English, philosophy, and world religions from the University of Colorado. She lives in Colorado with her Yorkshire Terrier.

---

1 For more on the oversoul, read *The Education of Oversoul Seven* by Jane Roberts, also my appendix "Meeting Oversoul in a Vision."

Also by Charol Messenger

THE NEW HUMANS (Series Book 2 "*The New Humanity*") – 2018 Second Edition. First Place Winner in Soul Bridge Book Awards of Europe 2017 in "Spiritual Awakening of Humanity." Second Place International Book Excellence Award (sole Finalist) in Body-Mind-Spirit.

HUMANITY 2.0 (Series Book 1 "*The New Humanity*") – 2018 Second Edition. Second Place Winner International Book Excellence Awards 2016 (sole Finalist) in Spirituality. National Finalist 2012 in *both* USA Best Books for New Age Nonfiction and CIPA EVVY in Spirituality. Third Place CIPA EVVY 2002 in Spirituality for the 1st Edition *The New Humanity* (replaced discontinued 2000 Xlibris edition) and is Vol. I in *Humanity 2.0* (all editions).

INTUITION FOR EVERY DAY (Series Book 3 "living your Higher Self") – 2018 Second Edition. Master Workbook on Enhancing Intuition. Meditations and techniques for: beginners, intermediate, and advanced. National Finalist USA Best Books 2015 in New Age Nonfiction.

YOU 2.0 (Series Book 2 "living your Higher Self") – 2018 Second Edition. Master Workbook on Higher Self initiation and integration. First Place Winner in International Book Excellence Awards 2016 in Personal Growth.

THE SOUL PATH (Series Book 1 "living your Higher Self") – 2018 Third Edition. Master Workbook on Becoming Fully Conscious. National Finalist USA Best Books 2015 in General Spirituality.

WINGS OF LIGHT (Series Book 1 "Angels") – 2018 Second Edition. Master Workbook on Connecting with the Four Angels Who Guide You. National Finalist CIPA EVVY 2012 in Spirituality.

WALKING WITH ANGELS (Series Book 2 "Angels") – 2018 Second Edition (in development, expanding, plus in print) (1st Ed. ebook retired).

I'M DANCING AS FAST AS I CAN (Series Book 1 Memoirs) – National Finalist USA Best Books 2005, memoir, vignette poetry.

All of the Messenger books include discussions of humanity's origin stories and evolution and our changing global society.

Contents

Part I: Everyday Intuition

Inner Hearing

The Still Small Voice Within, Sixteen Personal Anecdotes, Focused Intent

The Men in Blue — Traffic Court — Jury Duty — Free Live Theater Tickets — My Lost Border Collie Dreamed to Me Where to Find Her ... Multiple Times — Crickets Listen Too — Falling Down a Flight of Concrete Steps and The Disembodied Voice Beside Me — Telepathy, An Inherent Ability

Intuitive Sensing

Empathy, Innate Human "Radar," *Nine Personal Anecdotes, Five Techniques, including Mind Energy Focus*

How I Moved a Tornado — How I Moved a Flash Flood — How a Friend Kept a Forest Fire from Her Mountain Home — How a Group of Friends Helped Move an Eastern Seaboard Hurricane Out to Sea — Calming Strong Winds

Inner Seeing

Thirty-seven Examples from over 20,500 Higher Self Clairvoyant spiritual soul readings, *Seventeen Techniques, Personal Anecdote*

Part II: Honing Your Intuition

Morning Jumpstart
How Do You Love Yourself?

Part III: Heightened Intuition

Appendices

INTUITION
FOR
EVERY DAY

Book 3 "Living your Higher Self" Series
Second Edition

Enhancing Intuition
Master Workbook

Charol Messenger

Always knowing what to do,
through your inherent inner wisdom.

The Awakening

The Divine Presence exuded through every cell of my being, nurturing every thought, attitude, and emotion. I had come out of a long inner darkness and a month of unexpected awakened intuitive abilities.

It was Sunday, November 2, 1975, two a.m. I was thirty years old, divorced, and living alone in my apartment in Colorado Springs, Colorado.

In the middle of this long dark night, a spontaneous mystical activation into cosmic consciousness shattered my self-image and transformed my sense of self, as if I had been picked up and set in the opposite direction.

My outpouring heart opened me to all the wisdom of the ages streaming into my consciousness. I poured myself wholly into the fullness of this new divine and ecstatic place of human beingness, and a tremendous euphoria filled me. I felt the grandeur of the Universal Consciousness—of which I then *knew* I was an integral part. For the first time, I had a sense of identity and a sense of purpose.

An irrepressible explosion of insight and wisdom whirled through me, transforming my small sense of self into something profound and larger. The world was suddenly filled with vibrant sounds, textures, images, and colors. Extra-ordinary grace expanded my imagination, hopes and desires, surpassing anything I had ever thought possible for my life. For the first time, I truly was stepping into, onto the edge of my future, my destiny.

Doubt succumbed to hope, possibility, potential, and all the extraordinary dreams that would keep me stretching. The shackles and blinders of my previous existence fell away and I saw my true life, the true world, and the true destiny of humanity and of each soul.

I saw the lights of every soul on earth. I saw us all transcending our small narrow lives, lifting up into our true light, our true nature. I saw who we really are: We are large. We are a grand species. We are individuals filled with the ideal Self.

It was in this revelatory moment, the culmination of many days of out-of-body visions and transcendent travels, that I knew why I was in this life, this world, this body.

The very next breath I took was the first breath of my new life. I breathed for the first time with the fullness of Spirit, with the heart of a gentle and valiant soul, with the mind of a seer and a teacher of wisdom, to remind us all who we really are. For we have always been this grand Self. None of us has ever stopped being this grand Self.

In this moment of my first breath, I saw the wholeness of us all. I saw our glad hearts. I saw and felt the smiles and laughter of our true Nature. I felt the yearning of our hearts for release from pain and anguish. I felt the cries of our true beings for peace and sanity. I felt the pull of all souls in the world to find a way to be reminded of their inner light, to find a way to rekindle that connection, to find a way to remember and once again live from that place of our deep Self that is sacred and free of all regret.

In that moment, Spirit set itself upon me. Spirit opened my heart, my mind, my eyes, my ears, my tongue; giving me gifts of knowing, knowledge of the inner worlds, knowledge of our true Selves, knowledge and understanding of what we are and what we once again can be, knowledge of where we are evolving as a people, knowledge of how to help individuals remember.

In this hour of awakening to my true Self, my destiny came upon me as a cloak of surrender, no matter what the cost; a cloak of sanctity to give all that I am to help the people of this world find even a moment or a glimpse of what I *knew* in this single hour.

Since that day, I have had many hours, at times many months, of uninterrupted bliss and a continuous glow in the rapture of the Divine Presence breathing its force through me, that I may fulfill my purpose—which is to rekindle the *memory* of what we all are: divine beings.

That tremendous surging Vital Force still pushes me to transcend my everyday reality and to continue to reach out—because that is how we grow, that is how we each have made it this far, how we have always evolved and become more as a people and as individuals.

Awakened to my divine Nature, the fullness of Spirit flooded my being, flushed, purged, and nurtured my every thought and feeling to be a voice of the Divine, a hand of the Divine, to share with others whatever the Divine gives through me.

Graced by the splendid touch of God, thereafter transformed, I gave over my life wholly to be of service. That was the beginning of my life and the opening of my journey into my heart.

We are the Divine. We are all precious. Every single one of us is a spark of the *Divine All Knowing Presence* we call God. God speaks through us every day—through our lives. That is what God is. God is *us* when we are being our wholeness.

Introduction

Being *conscious* is living intuitively.

Intuition is innate in every human being. It is instinct and gut feeling, and works like "human radar."

Intuition is the ability to know what to do in any situation: to sense probable outcomes and consequences of your actions; to know when and when not to be concerned about something, whether to participate in an activity, whether to pursue a particular relationship (and whether as a lover, mate, friend, acquaintance, or business associate).

Heightened intuition is a benefit of spiritual balance, an *effect*. Spiritual balance is balancing *all* aspects of your being. Heightened intuition is the *first lesson* in becoming conscious, and is the *first indicator* of higher attainment. To enhance your natural, inborn intuition:

- Trust your instincts (guidance system, inborn radar).
- Trust yourself, that you *do* know what you're doing.
- Trust the spiritual forces that guide you (Higher Self, Spirit, angels).
- Be authentic (true to yourself).
- Be willing to be spontaneous.
- Use common sense. (e.g., don't jump off a bridge, unless you are bungee-jumping)
- Listen to the inner nudgings.
- Accept what feels right, and heed it.
- Take the one step you *are* sure of right now.
- When a new idea occurs to you, take that step.
- Then another idea occurs to you. Take that step...

When we act on what we know in the moment, our mind is free to see the next step.

Our mind is clear and receptive *after* we let go of worrying about a decision and simply trust our instincts.

Everything else follows, as you need it.

It isn't what others do to us
that creates our state of mind.

It is our state of mind
that creates what others do to us.

Part I

Everyday Intuition

INNER HEARING

EVERYDAY USE AND SAFETY

The still small voice within is our soul guiding us.

The Men in Blue

I was driving home from Denver to Colorado Springs, an hour-and-a-half trip south on I-25. When approaching my neighborhood on this Tuesday evening at eleven p.m., I was very tired. On the spur of the moment, I decided to stop at the Dunkin' Donuts on my left.

After pulling back out of the small shopping center, with my treat in the bag, I waited at the very long traffic light. Several minutes passed. It was late and there was absolutely no traffic—so I decided to go through the red light and make the left turn home only six blocks away.

Words immediately popped into my mind: *Why don't you turn right, then make a u-turn?*

That would have been legal, I realized. However, typically contrary and stubborn, I said aloud to myself, "Now, why should I do that?" So I did as I wanted, pulled through the red light, and turned left.

As soon as I was in the right lane headed home, a police car pulled up behind me, with its red and blue lights flashing in the dark night.

When the uniformed officer came up to my window, which I rolled down, the first thing he said was, "Why didn't you turn right, then make a u-turn?"

I was stunned! *Wow!*

Well, I'd been warned. He gave me a ticket.

Traffic Court

A few weeks later, I decided to take that ticket to court, because the traffic light had been inordinately slow and there had been no traffic, so I felt somewhat justified in driving through the red light.

While sitting in the cubicle in front of the young assistant district attorney, I was very nervous. I had meditated beforehand and now held my *focus of intention,* the true outcome I desired: to receive fair treatment but a reduced sentence. Holding my *focus of intention*, I visualized in my mind's eye and felt an *energy sensation:* I saw my crown chakra open and a column of clear light straight up to my Higher Self. In my heart and mind, I genuinely let go and was willing to accept whatever treatment I would be given.

I then stated my story to the Assistant D.A., without any effort or force of will.

Much to my amazement, just as the young fellow was about to reduce my traffic points from four to two—holding his pen in the air just above the page, just about to write—he changed his mind right then and wrote *zero* and told me to tell the judge the same story. So I did.

On my way into the courtroom, I knew the fee could be as much as seventy-five dollars, at least twenty-five (which was a great deal of money for me at that time, but mentally I decided ten dollars would be fair).

Standing before the judge, with my knees shaking, I told my story (during which entire time, I continued to hold the visualization of the white light up to Spirit and my clear intention *for the highest good of all* ... still affirming in my heart the outcome I preferred).

After hearing my story, the judge ordered me to pay *ten dollars.* I was stunned ... and relieved.

This *focused intention* stuff was powerful!

The secret:

- Ask for what you want.
- Hold the focus.
- Release the outcome.
- Don't worry.
- Don't demand.
- Accept the highest good for all.

Here's another example of mental telepathy while driving my car. I was going south from Colorado Springs on a long business trip all the way to Waco, Texas, a seventeen-hour drive. I was alone, in my twenty-year-old junker, a white 1972 Mercury Comet.

Out on the open highway, approaching Trinidad, Colorado, I felt free—as I always do behind the wheel on a road trip, one of the great benefits of living in America. I mentally visualized a bubble of white light around my old car for safety, then I asked the angels to watch over me and keep me safe on this long trip. My speed accelerated, and I was feeling good.

The other side of the freeway was some distance away across a very wide gulch. Before I had asked for the protection, I had seen three highway patrol cars pass me in the opposite direction, way over there. Now as soon as I asked the angels to look out for me and keep me safe, amazingly a fourth police car—way over there across the gulch—drove over the gulch, straight at me. When he gave me only a warning ticket for speeding, I counted myself lucky and cautioned.

Jury Duty

While *focused intent* has been very helpful regarding driving my car, it also has kept me off jury duty, twice. Again, I did not force it. I followed the same technique as with the Assistant D.A. who dropped my traffic points to zero.

I was sitting in the jury box and being questioned. All I did was hold my focus of intention *for the highest good of all.* I felt and visualized my column of light up through the top of my head to Spirit.

Mentally I stated my preference to myself: not to be a juror (because I was concerned about losing income for days away from my home business and sole source of income). The judge dismissed me.

The second time I was called to jury duty, I was one of four alternates not called to the box for questioning. We waited in the courtroom seats. Holding the Spirit connection, again I released all worry and concern and accepted whatever outcome—yet I received what I mentally *asked* for (dismissal from jury duty) and got it.

Free Live Theater Tickets

Focused intention comes in handy for FUN stuff, too. It was the 1980s and I was living in Colorado Springs. Being a full-time freelance intuitive reader, I was usually poor financially (living the "artist's" life). Yet I deeply wanted to see the off-Broadway show *Cats* that was coming to town. I never spent money on such luxuries, certainly not forty dollars.

I decided to try something new and put out the desire *mentally* that a ticket would come to me, that someone would *give* me a ticket (although this had never happened before and I had no reason now to believe that it would). As a test, I didn't tell anyone. Since I really didn't feel anything would happen, I dismissed the thought.

The week of the show, a woman visiting from out of town called me. She had just seen my business card for intuitive readings at the Windows of Light bookstore in Manitou Springs, a small community in the foothills of the Rocky Mountains west of Colorado Springs. She was a performer in the off-Broadway tour of *Cats*!

"Would you like to see the show?" she asked. She wasn't even looking to get a reading. She just wanted to give me a ticket.

"Yes!" I said, and cried.

My seat was front-row center, in addition to an extra seat for my girlfriend, Jan, a co-worker at my last real job as a word processor at the International Typographical Union, the job I started in January 1976 right after my awakening. The performer, Donna Lee, was the lead singer, playing the part of Grizelda. When Donna Lee sang

"Memories," her splendid crystal clear voice resonated through me and moved me to tears.

After the show, Donna Lee invited Jan and me to visit with her and the cast. We all sat at Denny's nearby for three hours. I was in heaven!

It turned out that Donna Lee was very much spiritually aware and interested in the healing arts. This was a very powerful evening for me. Even better than I had hoped ... and much better than I had asked for.

That's how it works. Good stuff, huh?

Did I say thank you to Donna Lee ... and to the Universe? I sure did. "THANK YOU!"

Another similar incident was a free ticket to the symphony. I was standing in line for a ticket. Although I had little money to spare, I very much wanted to attend to soothe my soul. A man came up to the Rush line and asked if anyone wanted a single free ticket.

"Me!"

My Lost Border Collie Dreamed to Me Where to Find Her ... Multiple Times

In the late 1970s, I had numerous telepathic communications with my tan border collie, Che. In the early days, as a puppy, she had been very difficult. She was high strung and barked a lot; being in an apartment didn't suit her abundant energy.

I had adopted Che at three months old. When she was one year old, I felt the need to give her away because she was so unhappy cooped up while I was away all day at a secretarial job. The family to whom I gave her lived in the mountains, had children, and seemed to be a good match for my dog. A few days after separating from Che, I left on a six-week round trip ticket via Amtrak through California and back. The entire time I was gone, I had nightmares about Che. I kept dreaming that she had been abandoned.

As soon as I returned home to Colorado Springs, I tried to locate the family to whom I had given her. Their phone was disconnected, which distressed me considerably because I was still having these terrible dreams.

My girlfriend Jan went with me to drive up into the mountains in Woodland Park where the family was supposed to live. When we arrived, the house was vacant.

Fortunately, a sign was posted on the property with the landlord's phone number. Jan and I went right over to see them and Che was there. The landlord's family had been keeping her.

Just as I had dreamed, the family to whom I had given Che had abandoned her. Right after I gave Che to them, they had packed and moved to California and left the dog alone inside the house they were renting—without food or water and without notifying anyone they had left her. When the landlord found Che, she had been locked up inside that house for several days and had pooped and peed all over.

Che seemed happy now with the landlord's family. They lived in a trailer and had children, horses and other pets. We agreed that they would keep Che. However, I stipulated that if they *ever* changed their minds, for any reason whatsoever, call me first and I would take her back. I felt a soul connection with this dog and responsible for her well-being; as long as she was happy, I knew it was okay to let them keep her. So, I left Che behind and all was well.

Two years later, just two weeks after I moved into a roomy two-story duplex, I got the call. They wanted to give Che back. I immediately got in my car and went back to get her. She stayed with me forever after that.

My bond with Che surpassed ordinary senses. Whenever I traveled—and left her with a dog sitter (at home to minimize her stress)—on my first night away from home, in a *dream* I always stopped in and checked on Che. Once I saw that she was all right, the rest of my trip would be fine and my dreams were normal.

Another incident with Che one summer was also quite remarkable. I attended a week-long retreat in the Black Forest, a wooded community just north of Colorado Springs, as part of an Edgar Cayce annual conference. During the two years while Che was gone, I had adopted a black tortoise-shell cat I named Gypsy (rather, she had adopted me). I left Gypsy alone inside the duplex, and I left Che at Jan's house. The first night I was away, I dreamed that I visited my home, the duplex. I saw the cat inside ... and I saw Che outside on the uncovered, back concrete porch.

When I woke and remembered the dream, while it seemed odd, I didn't *feel* worried. Nevertheless, I meditated on it; I was at the retreat and feeling very spiritually connected. Everything still felt really okay, so I trusted what I *felt* and I didn't call Jan (although I should have, and I would these days).

As good fortune would have it, my dream turned out to be true, as well as my intuition. The first day at Jan's house, Che had dug under their backyard fence and run away. After work that day, Jan had stopped at my duplex and Che was there—on the porch—although I had never visited Jan's house before and never had taken Che there. Although the distance from my duplex near downtown Colorado Springs and Jan's house north of the city was a forty-five minute drive, Che had somehow found her way home. When Jan arrived (God bless her), Che was lying on my porch in my unfenced yard. Jan decided to leave her at my house, tied up every day, and check on her after work, because the summer weather was mild. Every evening, Jan checked on Che and left her food and water.

Just as I had dreamed, Che was at my home—not where I had left her. And just as I had dreamed, all *was* well and I didn't need to worry (which I hadn't). Still, these days I would have more common sense and confirm with a phone call, rather than leave it up to chance.

Telepathy is great. It relieves all need to worry. You can just *feel* that all is well (just like you can feel when there is danger). It's pretty neat.

That isn't the end of the Che stories. One September a few years later, Che passed over from this world at the age of fifteen. I grieved for her as if I had lost a child, but it was time to put her to sleep. She was suffering too much from old age, was in a great deal of pain, and having a very difficult time breathing. That December, three months later, I dreamed that Che visited me and was coming back as a new collie puppy, telling me where she would be born and asking if I wanted her back. She would be born in February, she said. I decided I wasn't ready and declined the invitation. The relationship had been difficult although I loved her dearly.

A floppy-eared miniature schnauzer had been with me and Che for several years now; they had bonded instantly and were best friends, even though Che was six years older than Cabra. I called them my Disney pair, because they loved frolicking together. (In the interim, Gypsy, my wonderful cat, had moved on to another home; she never did get used to having a dog around. She didn't want to share me.)

Sweetheart Cabra, the schnauzer, instead of grieving over the loss of her best friend, Che, nurtured *me* and made sure that *I* got enough love. Dogs are selfless souls.

Crickets Listen, Too

I have insect stories, too. Ants and flies listen pretty well if you tell them to leave. Mosquitoes, in my case, don't. Nor do wasps. I did once have a whole "family" of ants depart the day I asked them to leave. That was cool. However, my favorite story is the cricket.

I was living in another two-level duplex, at the foot of Cheyenne Mountain, where NORAD is (the same place used in the Sci-Fi cable series *SG-1.* Both Che and Cabra were my family.

On the main floor, off the large open living-dining room I had a full-sized washer and dryer. I kept hearing this cricket "singing." Finally I had enough and very clearly commanded it to leave. At the same time, I *happened* to also visualize the cricket departing and I was *emoting* a strong desire to be rid of the constant "music."

Within an hour or so, while I was watching TV, out came the cricket from behind the washer and dryer. As the weather was mild and warm, I had left the sliding glass door open a bit. The cricket came straight forward from the washer and dryer, made a sharp left turn in the living room and headed straight through the crack in the open door. Just like that!

Crickets are cool. Jiminy Cricket always was my favorite cartoon character. Now I knew why.

Falling Down a Flight of Concrete Steps — and the Disembodied Voice Beside Me

Being able to hear telepathically once even healed a serious physical injury of mine. At the same Cheyenne Mountain duplex, I slipped on the stairs to my downstairs, garden-level bedroom, bouncing on my butt all the way down the six steps, and landed hard on the concrete floor. *Plop!*

Stunned and motionless, immediately I heard an *audible* voice beside me on my left, as clear as if a human being was standing there—but *invisible.* I was astonished!

"Charol, be still. Stay where you are. Don't move."

Somehow I knew the voice was Alexandra, my spirit friend/muse who was as real to me as anyone I had ever known, like a sister. Today she became more real than I had ever imagined possible. The *physical voice* startled me, so I obeyed.

Alexandra patiently talked me through the crisis, advising me step by step what to do, which I followed implicitly. After all, I was *audibly* hearing every word spoken by this invisible person (a nonphysical person, not an angel).

I slowly gathered myself up off the concrete floor, dragged myself up the stairs, and reclined face up on the sofa in the living room, as instructed. I *felt* Alexandra place etheric crystals and healing stones over my body in various places as she described to me (now *mentally*) what she was doing. I *felt* the energy of the various gemstones and remained in a restful state. This treatment took several hours. At the end of the process, when Alexandra advised, I went to bed.

I had no after-effects or injuries from this fall down the stairs, not even bruises. I was normal. (Well, as normal as ever.)

Telepathy, An Inherent Ability

These are just a few examples of how telepathy can be very practical. The lesson, of course, is: LISTEN to the thoughts coming *into* your mind *to* you.

Telepathy is our natural human radar. It comes in many forms: thoughts, feelings, hunches, instincts, intuitions, gut reactions.

Telepathy is the *inner knowing* that bugs you.

Not recognizing a telepathic ability in oneself is only from not yet *perceiving* it; and the perception is *learned,* through the inner communion.

The better telepath you are, the better life works—because you are more conscious about what you are doing and less at the mercy of whims, urges, and habits.

This *heightened* awareness becomes more sensitive with use. How quickly you activate this skill depends on the subconscious maturity you already have accomplished. However, not being conscious yet of your spiritual insight does not mean you may not already have a telepathic ability. You may simply not have *activated* it yet.

So, how do you awaken your telepathic ability?

By living up to your potential, pursuing your dreams, actualizing your goals, and living with an attitude of: for the common good and the free will of all.

These techniques also help: meditation, affirmations (state of mind), self-hypnosis (as with guided audio exercises), writing down your dreams, studying areas of metaphysics or esotericism that appeal to you.

Mainly, stay with positive and constructive activities and avoid people, movies, books, and activities that bring you down.

Hearing thoughts spoken *into* your mind can be learned. It takes realizing and accepting that the thoughts coming *to* you are real.

Three Simple Steps to Hearing Your Inner Guide

Soul uses the inner voice to guide us.

We communicate with our inner guide through being *still.* Awareness comes in listening. How do you do that?

Open your heart to the light of Spirit. If you don't hear the still, small inner voice, release. If you don't always experience meditations as you wish, don't judge what you are receiving. Accept whatever you *do* experience. That is the secret of spiritual expansion. It comes subtly during our committed process.

I have found that the secret to heightened awareness is to be grateful for every glimmer of insight, every moment of bliss. It is through gratitude that we grow a compassionate heart, through which we discover our connection to all of life.

To strengthen your connection, it helps to voice-record what you experience during meditation (saying aloud what you see, feel, hear, sense).

The language of soul comes in pictures, thoughts, and feelings and this requires being open and receptive. It's a heart link, not a mental link. So be patient with the journey. Awareness is a process. Awareness evolves.

Tip: Meditate without expectation. You may have moments of rapture and *feel* the *force* in you. You may only feel peaceful. You will at some point receive insights.

We hear the inner voice in the *stillness,* and reach the stillness through deep breathing,. Through breath, we connect with our higher mind and relate with our inner counselor.

Breath is the key. To focus your breath, following are three simple steps.

Simple Step 1

Sit quietly, without distracting sounds. Be still and listen to your breath.

- Feel your breath flowing in and out. Invite the breath. Absorb it.

- Become aware now of your innermost thoughts, the soft inner voice coming into your awareness, the thoughts being sent *to* you.

Simple Step 2

- Breathe deeply, to let go of all anticipation.

- Merely feel the *stillness* within you. An inner thought comes to you. It comes *into* your consciousness from *outside* your mind. It is a thought transmitted that you receive mentally.

- Be still now and again hear the voice. Be still for a long time. Just listen and get used to it. Get used to hearing this *still, small voice.*

- Now relax and trust the inner voice advice. Perceive the advice as inspiration, insight, vision, the presence of the Divine. Expect nothing in particular. Merely listen.

What should you do if you are asked to do something in particular by the inner voice? You have the *free will* to act or not act upon any advice given. Nothing is commanded of us. You are free to *choose.*

We learn to evaluate the clarity of the insights by applying them whenever we feel they are nonthreatening to our lifestyle and others.

More useful teachings come when we *live* the insights given to us from the clear inner mind. Until then, it is helpful to study all religions, philosophies, and avenues of spiritual growth.

You may wish to write the words you hear into a notebook in your lap, as you hear them, or repeat them into a recorder.

By this latter process (telepathic inner dictation from the higher mind), I wrote over two dozen books, including all of the meditations and techniques in this book.

Mind energy cannot be contained. Mind is not limited by dimensions or space. We bridge the vastness of the cosmic planes by having an open mind and open expectation.

This unexpected method motivated me to strive toward discovering *how* to integrate my own eternal soul power, in a practical and meaningful way, and to learn to live as a soul-embodied human ... which is a work in progress.

Simple Step 3

Take twenty minutes daily, preferably mornings, to be silent and still:

- Be still. Breathe deeply. Do nothing else ... until you become aware of the consciousness and the life force within you.

- Perceive light. See light coming into you. Feel light radiating through you and warming you. Feel its universal power within you.

- Feel your heart glowing, love overflowing and filling you ... until you are love.

- To know your soul ... listen. Be still and listen. Be still and *know.*

You can safely practice these exercises on your own.

I also highly recommend any materials by Jonathan Parker of Gateways Institute, Wayne Dyer, and Dick Sutphen.

Another way to learn rhythmic breathing is to take courses with practitioners who offer breath work, such as hatha yoga. Guided exercises on cassette or CD, including self-hypnosis, are also very helpful.

Once you have learned rhythmic breathing, prepare a place to do meditations. When you waken during the night, get up and go sit in that place.

The inner voice is quiet, heard in the stillness of the breath. Hearing one word at a time is common at first. It takes practice. Practice leads to hearing the inner voice at any time of the day (after a while).

By considerable personal effort, you can learn to believe in your ability to discern, test, try, and live by the insights that *come* to you—which can free you from fears and illusions. By stepping ahead in the sojourn of your heart and spirit, you can access the Universal Mind.

The Universal Mind, another name for the Akashic Records, is all whole perceptions of life. When you are dedicated to the process of being whole and you are committed to the light (essential qualifications for anyone seeking to help humanity), you are able to tap the Consciousness.

Your identification with being a student of light—one seeking increased self-awareness—opens within you a bridge to receive personal counsel and tutoring along the way of life's explorations.

When you touch God deep in your being, you know.

INTUITIVE SENSING

We affect everyone around us—by our actions, body language, facial expressions, gestures, tone of voice.

Our emotions and thoughts project around us continuously. We can't get away from who we are. Everyone knows us.

Our only hope for peace of mind is to be the best person we can be right now, today. Then no matter what happens, we know we gave our best.

That's all anyone can do, and that's all you have to do, just your best.

EARTH ANGEL

An angel visited me one day, through the unexpected counsel of someone who came for an intuitive reading. She was from out of town and the sister of a kind man I had worked for ten years prior. Although I was in the throes of flu and vertigo, I agreed to do a short session.

Mary, seventy-five, had white hair and knew that her time left on Earth was short. We bonded quickly at a deep soul level. The reading was brief but poignant and true to the heart. When we finished, I realized I had been psychically clear even though my body was ill. I then realized I could rise above the conditions of the body and still do what was needed.

Mary looked into my eyes and said, "Now, you're not going to be afraid any longer, are you?"

As she spoke, I felt the hand of Soul, Teacher, angel, on my heart—whoever watches over us and sends us counselors in our everyday world to ease our struggles. And so, once again, were renewed my strength and my belief.

After Mary left, I wondered, *What makes us feel vulnerable?* How had I become inundated by fear? How had I become overwhelmed by lethargy, indecision, confusion? How could I release these? How could I know the right thing to do?

The inner answer came: *How do you **feel**?*

We are in light when we *listen* to our feelings and acknowledge our discomfort but accept our instinctual *knowing* which may require change.

First, listen to your feelings. If a situation gives you a feeling of being drained, confused, fearful or nullified, something about that situation may not be right for you (at least not at the time). However, if a situation feels natural, pleasant, inspiring and rejuvenating, it may be right for you ... at this time.

Feelings are your best cue. Feelings are your own real testimony. Feelings can guide you—to and away.

Humans are naturally intuitive. We are naturally psychic, empathic, and telepathic. It's who we are. Every one of us.

Acknowledging your *feelings* is a basic survival tool.

To transcend fear—even the fear that you can't, or shouldn't do something—*feel* your needs ... and *whatever* your needs are, know they are right for you.

How can you know what to do about something? How can you rise above mental confusion? How can you let go?

Listen to your feelings (gut instincts, emotional reaction, sensitivity to energy, physical symptoms). Do what makes you feel comfortable.

If something makes you feel happy and whole, it is right for *you.* On the other hand, if something makes you feel uncomfortable, it is a wrong choice for *you*—person, place, thing, idea, opportunity. Even concepts and ideals can be misleading, so it is important to listen to what *feels* right for you.

Soul has repeatedly told me, *Life is meant to be enjoyed.* When we get lost in fear or pain, or resist what our feelings are urging us to do, we are not living in harmony. My solution for my own vulnerabilities is to listen to my *inner knowing.*

Soul continuously talks to us, guiding us in every moment—by what we feel and know in our *center.* The communication of the *inner knowing self* is very subtle. Think of it as a *guidance system,* an innate *radar* system that is inborn in being human, is always there and has always been there: to help us through this world, find what will make us truly joyful, and give us the feeling of being blessed and in the right place at the right time.

That comes from listening to our heart and feeling our center, our gut instinct; trusting that it must be true, and acting upon what we *know* in that moment.

You know what is right *in the moment.* We seldom have any more information than that. The secret is to act on *what* you know right now. The rest will follow.

What steps to take will occur to you *after* you commit, *after* you decide. That's when the mind and heart become free of worry (the mental merry-go-round) so you are able to receive fresh insights that just *occur* to you. And you think, "Wow. It's so easy. Why didn't I think of that before?"

It is easy. Trusting yourself—trusting the inner sensing of what is right to do (when logic, peers, status quo may indicate otherwise) is the hardest part. Get that and the rest will follow naturally. The hardest part is trusting your instincts (instead of the "what ifs" rolling around in your head).

Trust your instincts—what you *know* you should do—and everything *will* work out ... like it's supposed to. This *rule* applies to everything in life—who to love (or not), whether to go (or stay), whether to move (where and when), this job (or if it's time to move on), whether to buy a new car now or wait. It takes *practice.* (For me, a lot of practice.)

When I forget (which does happen), I am reminded by something "magical" in my life. For example, my instincts nagged at me for a year on an idea. The idea kept working on me and wouldn't let go. It wouldn't go away. Finally one day it got so intense that I found myself flowing with it. The thought just kept going round and round and round in my head: *I should be able to get an investor to finance my book, The New Humanity. I should be able to get someone to finance it.* I knew that investors were supposed to be next to impossible to get. However, I had learned a long time ago (the first time the *magic* happened, when I gave my first intuitive reading and didn't know I was going to or even could) that when I "flow," *magic* happens and I find myself able to do something that never before occurred to me.

On a Sunday in January 2001, once again I flowed. Once I let go, the idea to get an investor carried itself and generated its own vitality. I just had to keep up. I found myself working on a letter to send to whoever I could think of to ask for money to publish one of my two dozen books, *The New Humanity.* My years of professional writing helped; I had an instinct for what needed to be said and how to say it. Nevertheless, I *was* asking for money.

Flushed with ideas, I ended up with a pretty comprehensive letter, detailing what I was asking for, what I believed would happen with the book, how I expected to generate sales, and what I would do for the investor in return.

I then made a list of people to contact. I did not allow any negative thoughts to stop the flow. I continued straight on. I faxed the proposal to the two top people on my list of eighteen, people who had believed in me in the past.

The first person I reached called me and sent a check the next day for $3,000 to print the book, and another $2,000 soon after to promote it. *That* was magic! (One week later, I attended a Small Business course on getting investment capital and was told it's pretty much impossible.)

I had met Keith, the man who financed *The New Humanity*, twenty years before. I had a lucid dream in the spring of 1980 to move to Lake Tahoe from Colorado, so I did. That summer, taking my border collie, Che, but leaving Gypsy, the cat, behind with a new family, I gave up my great downtown two-story duplex (the one where Che had stayed outside all week while I was away on the Edgar Cayce retreat).

Three months after moving to Tahoe, I moved back to Colorado Springs because I couldn't figure out how to make a living (I wasn't assertive enough then to earn my keep as an intuitive reader or as a freelance editor). I moved all my furniture to California, and back, in a U-Haul. Yet the truth was, if I hadn't actually *moved* (and not just vacationed), I wouldn't have met Keith. He was a friend of the woman from whom I rented a small cottage near South Lake Tahoe on the Nevada side. He and I dated and stayed in touch after I left. I made another short visit the summer of 1983. He visited me in Colorado a couple of times over the years when he was traveling. That was it.

Isn't life amazing? Yes, it is.

Such moments as this have kept me going and hopeful, reminding me that there is a Higher Power at work and to simply trust my life to it. I seem to need a lot of reminding though. The hardest part of life, for me, is holding onto my vision when everything takes so darned long to happen. It's moments when the *magic* does happen— like the heavens opening up and light pouring in and all the angels singing—that I know there *is* a reason for the waiting, even though I can't see the reason at the time. Living in Spirit requires faith—in yourself and in the Bigger Picture that you may not fully see.

The *inner knowing* is how we connect with Spirit and how Spirit connects with us. It doesn't matter what names or labels we use to identify this *connection* or what Spirit is. All that matters is that we find a way to listen to it, a way to learn to trust it, and the courage to act upon whatever *knowing* fills us. That's when we are at-one with God.

We all have this *knowing.* We all have access to it. The *knowing* is what guides us ... and it always works. We just have to allow the Universe to fulfill its plan, of which we seldom know all the pieces: the when, the why, the who. All we know is *what* will happen.

PREMONITIONS AND FOREBODINGS

Our bodies are sensitive to energy forces in the environment, seen and unseen, even though we are seldom aware of them. The body is a sensory system, and it reacts. It is, therefore, important to identify your reactions and observe your feelings, impressions, thought processes, and flashes of intuition.

The aura, an extension of the physical body, is a sensory mechanism. It feels and is aware of everything around it. The aura is like a computer. It takes input all the time and is constantly aware. Space and distance make no difference. Our being and mind are able to reach across miles to feel an impending danger *and* stop it.

How I Moved a Tornado

A grave sense of danger gripped me and pervaded every fiber of my being. I froze and began to sweat and gasp for breath. A sudden news flash on my Walkman radio was announcing a tornado whipping through my neighborhood right then in Northglenn, forty-five minutes away from my downtown Denver high-rise office where I was working as a temp secretary.

Yet what I felt was not ordinary fear. I had never felt a sensation like this before. Something deep inside me told me this was critical and that something catastrophic was about to happen. I gazed out the seventeenth-floor office window to the far horizon north.

The suburb where I lived with Ray was twenty miles away and I had taken the express RTD bus to work. My border collie, Che, was in the fenced backyard and my timid miniature schnauzer, Cabra, was loose in the house (all three of us had moved in with Ray, from

Colorado Springs). I couldn't get home in time to move the dogs to safety into the basement. Ray was out in the field with his Public Service utilities job and I couldn't reach him.

Anxiety compressed me! I had to do *something.* There must be something I could do!

Suddenly it *came* to me: *Invoke the power of the Universe and call on the angels for protection.*

Without any thought of how ridiculous I might look, hidden behind the high gray walls of my private cubicle workstation as a long-term temp, five months on the job, I invoked the protection and projected it from my mind's eye to the site of danger. I prayed to the Universe, to God, the angels, Archangel Michael, whoever might hear me (hoping they were all as real as I believed), asking for guidance and protection of my dogs, Ray, the house and all within it.

The protection ritual came *into* my mind step by step. I followed it spontaneously, just *knowing* what to say and do, guided as to what words to command, what images to visualize, and what physical gestures to project the protecting energy force toward our home.

I then left the cubicle for the privacy of the Ladies Room. There, amidst sanitary steel and ceramic, I thrust my arms into the air and, in a whispered tone, powerfully *commanded* and *directed* the protecting energy to my dogs and home.

I continued this ritual for about fifteen minutes. Suddenly the task felt *complete* and a calm contentment washed through me. I felt relaxed and at ease. Feeling totally free of concern, I returned to my cubicle and my work.

I truly released the outcome to the Universe, knowing I had done all I could and could do no more. I had invoked the forces of the Universe. I was resolved to *any* outcome, although I felt clearly that all *was* well. I felt comfortable, calm, and at peace; so I resumed my work tasks and gave no more real thought to the matter. It was one p.m.

When I returned home by bus at the end of the work day, my strong premonition proved to be true. I immediately ran through the house, grabbed up my floppy-eared Cabra and hugged her. Carrying my silver schnauzer in my arms, I hurried into the backyard. Che, my tan border collie, came crawling out of her doghouse, which was still in the same place as it was before in the yard. She was soaking wet but unharmed. She panted and her brown eyes were very big.

I turned and perused the yard. The tornado's path was visible. It had indeed touched down in our block. The debris and *lack* of damage startlingly revealed the tornado's journey. It had swept *up* right *over* our backyard, skipped *up* at the west fence, then dipped back down at the east fence, tearing out that fence but not damaging any part of our yard, including the wooden dog house only three feet away. From the east fence, the gusting tornado had ripped a trail right through the neighbor's back lawn.

According to the six o'clock TV news, the tornado had touched down in our exact block as it sped toward the railroad tracks only half a block east ... during the exact same fifteen minutes I was inner directed to send the protecting energy force.

Well, I surely believed in the Power then.

We are all connected through mind and energy, including to the earth and elements of nature. That is how the natural mental protection works. That is why we can indeed protect ourselves and our loved ones—by using the clearly directed power of our inner mind and inner will.

When we study with a regular discipline and daily apply ourselves to oneness with the Divine, we can be ready and prepared for any crisis. Intuitively and instinctively we can respond without a conscious recollection of how we know what to do.

We are able to fully defend our being, environment, and loved ones from circumstances that seem beyond anyone's control. No matter how devastating a circumstance appears to be, how it affects each person is individual. We definitely can eliminate real danger, because everything is energy and is directed by mind.

Mental energy is the web of life that ties us all together and to all the elements in life. When we are clear and centered, in a moment of crisis or impending danger, all of our learned resolve comes to bear effortlessly and instinctively. As if we consciously invoked it, we are filled with a knowing and inimitable power to dissolve danger—by our focused thoughts and aligned energy presence.

When we live in sync with our higher divine will and we daily practice disciplines of mind and spirit (to manage our emotions and impulses), we can take on a mature perception toward the life forces and our connection with them. We become one with them in our *intentions* toward life.

In the midst of storms and natural disasters, without fear and with complete presence, we can invoke—without question—our full powerful Stature. Our whole Self knows life, is one with nature, and is aligned in clarity and balance. When our whole Self commands nature, nature obeys, because both are a part of the basic structure of physical existence: energy.

How I Moved a Flash Flood

A swift, rushing flash flood deluged my entire neighborhood— except for *my* half of the Cheyenne Mountain duplex. It flooded my neighbor's basement, as well as all the houses around me.

At eleven p.m., while I was ironing in the living room, a flash-flood warning came on the TV, instructing everyone in my neighborhood to evacuate immediately. I stopped in the middle of ironing and began running around a bit crazily, grabbing up things to put in the car: computer disks and volumes of as yet unpublished manuscripts. Then I looked frantically about the office at all of my important stuff. There was no way I could take everything that really mattered to me, a lifetime of creative materials I still planned to publish.

At that moment, a sudden clarity and assuredness overcame me and I found myself declaring—with all knowing and might—"It just can't be!"

Instinctively, I pulled up into my full height, stretching and filling with my old-soul warrior presence. My emotions centered to a dead calm, my mind cleared, and my thoughts sharpened to laser efficiency.

I spun through the room, then the entire house, diligently declaring, "IT WILL NOT BE!"

Like a shaman, I drew on an instinctual subliminal soul memory and stormed throughout my two-story home. I thrust my arms upward and outward, room by room, projecting a force-field bubble of white light around the house, visualizing it clearly in my mind's eye; thrusting outward the innate cosmic power in all directions, and *commanding* the flood waters AWAY. With the full splendor of my TOTAL BEING and with clear intention, I willed—in words, thoughts, and images—the waters to travel *around* my home ... and I *saw* the area fully protected.

Suddenly the task felt *complete* and a calm contentment washed over me. The energy was set and I knew that I, Che and Cabra, our home, and all within were safe. I went back to ironing and watching TV without any further thought on the matter. In fact, I forgot all about the flood. It escaped my mind.

The next day, my half of the duplex was the only residence in my entire extended neighborhood for several blocks around that did not get flooded. My duplex neighbor's garden-level basement was flooded. Mine was dry.

I had overlooked only one item in my shaman ritual. When visualizing the waters going *around* my home, I had neglected to include in my mental picture the little fenced side yard that held my large heavy wooden doghouse. The flood waters had torn open the fence in several places and pushed the dog house twenty feet forward. But my home and my car in the front gravel driveway were dry ... the only dry spot for miles around.

How a Friend Kept a Forest Fire from Her Mountain Home

Using the Mind Energy Focus

The following true story happened March 2011, with a friend of mine in Golden, Colorado. Here are our email letters. She is Miss B.

3/21/11:

MISS B: "We have a forest fire in Golden, about 10 miles from me."

ME: "I noticed that late last night on TV... I thought of you... Oh, my. KEEP SAFE. Sending a white light shield around you. RIGHT NOW. You do it, too. Visualize............. all around you. VISUALIZE... BOLDLY."

MISS B: "If those winds pick up, we could be looking at a very significant fire in the foothills. I already have my bags packed and will head to my daughter's if we get the message to evacuate. Right now, only one subdivision down the hill is in the path, but who knows with the winds. It is so dry out there!"

ME: "Trust Your Gut Instincts... If you need help... the tornado and flood stories in my workbook emailed to me. GO WITH YOUR GUT."

MISS B: "Thanks, I remember those stories and, yes, I have previously taken your advice (especially with thunderstorms!), will do so again. Thanks."

ME: "It works especially well against real physical threats. I just finished a strong meditation. I'll go back IN and send help. Let me know what happens. The KEY: BE A WARRIOR. This is the time to pull out all the stops!"

MISS B: "Warrior B! This fire isn't going to get me!"

ME: [smiling]: "Yes, I 'saw' that. While creating the vacuum and safety around you, suddenly I 'saw' you being the warrior and I literally guffawed out loud. It was a very real gut feeling, wonderful! My Yorkie even jumped up in my lap! ... Warrior is absolutely the attitude that gets it done ...Breathe..."

MISS WARRIOR B: "Breathing...."

ME: email title "COOL ... Create (visualize and hold the image) a vacuum of safety and calm around you, your being, your body, around each of your dogs, around your car, around and above and over your entire house and property, extend it beyond your property on all sides, and beyond at least the next neighbor over. Everything included in your imaging is in the zone of protection. I 'see' it. I am holding it for you, too. You are the strongest voice for your own being and all around you. You are safe. Believe it. Know it. Then do what must be done. [e.g. be practical]"

3/22/11:

ME: email title "SAFE" ... "This 8:58 a.m., this inner message spontaneously came to me about you: 'B is safe.' All day yesterday, through the night (while asleep), still there this morning, and reinforced in a just-now meditation: Holding the vision (and feeling/seeing the power cord/light up through the crown of the head into the heavens, which expands the force field of protection out around it like a vortex, a zone of safety). You, your home and all within it, your entire property (including power lines, etc.), and expanding around to include all neighbors, and expanding surrounding as far as you can see. I 'see' the fire contained, on the other side of the hill (and that all that you can see remains green and alive). I 'see' containment poured all around it (e.g., circle) AND I spontaneously 'saw' the ground within that circle charred to the ground and out cold (and no houses within it). Hold the visions (hold the energy up through the crown). Let me know how you are."

MISS WARRIOR B: "I am indeed safe. I woke up to snow on the ground! It was not forecast at all [e.g., exceptionally dry this year]. It is like a blanket of protection for my home and the surrounding mountain where I live... What a wonderful gift!"

ME: "Oh, my God, that is so COOL. Ha. It really is COOL!!! WOW.

I'm so happy for you! And still hold the vision (and see/feel it up through your crown/top of head like a beacon of light into the heavens, the source of the centrifugal force sending out around you.... until it's really the cold damp spot (charred) on the other side of the hill.... and no houses in it.... just the earth.... (I will, too)."

The Indian Gulch Fire took from Monday through Saturday March 26, 2011 to put out. Winds were hurricane force for three to four days, gusting up to 75 mph, and dry conditions are "drought." The fire never crossed over the hill.

Coincidence? Or is focused intent powerful enough to move the forces of nature?

I believe that human beings have this innate ability. We simply forgot how... and we can relearn how to tap it... how to draw on it, when we are in danger. All I know is I have many personal stories of how it apparently did keep me out of harm's way. That's a good enough reason to keep using it, I believe.

Forest Fire Update — June 29, 2012
During a rash of Colorado wildfires and the two worst in Colorado's history

MISS B: "I am so thankful to be able to live in Colorado, in the foothills, with great views and wonderful nature. But nature here also brings danger, as we have seen during the 2012 summer lightning storms that have sparked devastating wildfires up and down the front range: Colorado Springs, Boulder, Fort Collins.

"With fires burning and destroying land and homes, when an early evening storm approached my area in those same foothills, I knew what to do. I remembered how last year [2011] I had seemingly stopped an approaching wildfire in early spring [got snow] by using what I knew about energy forces [learned from Charol]—and this time, also, I immediately got to work using that same technique.

"As the lightning strikes grew stronger and closer, I went to my deck overlooking the storm and waved my arms up to the heavens and around to the side, over and over; while imagining my own energy growing outward and upward, like a shield, to protect my house.

"I continued this, feeling my energy leave my body and go upward from my head. I verbally commanded it to protect and envelop my area, even my entire foothills neighborhood.

"I continued this again and again—feeling very strong and powerful—for about ten or fifteen minutes. And then, to my surprise, I felt raindrops! At first, just a few. Then the heavens opened up with a soaking rainstorm.

"Last year, it was snow. Now it was a protective rain—which was unpredicted and a huge surprise to weather forecasters. Not to me, though.

"Imagine if we all concentrated and projected our energy to protect our land, our property, our state, our country during impending danger. What power we all have!" ~ Miss B

How a Group of Friends Helped Move an Eastern Seaboard Hurricane Out to Sea

Using Mind Energy Focus,
resulting in unexpected minimal damage

Coincidence or...?

Hurricane Irene August 2011 was reported to advance up the entire eastern seaboard of the United States, including New York City. It was a dire warning from the tip of Florida all the way up into Nova Scotia, Canada.

While watching the news on TV, and seeing the entire coast line covered in red, the projected potential disaster zone, it occurred to me, for the first time ever, to focus energy to help ward off the hurricane or at least minimize its effects. I had not thought of such an action before, for any other disaster, and the feeling did not repeat itself for any subsequent natural disasters. This was the first time I had felt moved to do something beyond my own personal life.

Maybe there was something about this one. I don't know. I only know that, in that moment, the following image came to me, so I did it. It was effortless and quite simple. So then I sent these brief instructions in an email to a small handful of people who might want to participate (the more, the better). I also posted it on my blog.

Let's mentally move Hurricane Irene.

- Visualize the entire U.S. east coast.

- Mentally move the entire energy field of the hurricane out into the ocean.

- Keep moving it until it dissipates.

- Repeat, repeat, repeat.

- Hold that image—continuously (in the back of the mind, every time you think of it)—until the event passes.

Who knows if this helped? Maybe it did. I do feel that many people made such "prayers." What I do know is that the consequences of the hurricane were much less severe than anticipated by all weather forecasts.

Irene was potentially a category 3 hurricane, expected to devastate the entire eastern seaboard. As the weather ensued, the direction of the storm was as expected, however the intensity was reported to be less.

Anderson Cooper on CNN reported, "A very different scene than we had anticipated.... A lot of people in New York city are breathing a sigh of relief.... Nowhere nearly as bad as it could have been [from Battery Park, NY].... Cannot explain why the winds did not get down to the surface.... [If so] would have been seen even worse problems [flooding from storm surge] than seeing now.... Storm damage not as bad as feared [Rhode Island]."

The storm had weakened to a category 1 and lower winds; it was still dangerous, but mitigated. At Long Island, NY, it was downgraded to a tropical storm and winds reduced to 65-75 and there was much less damage than expected.

The storm had initially changed at North Carolina, and Anderson Cooper reported, "the best possible outcome" as the storm lost its "mojo."

Right after I sent the email to a few contacts, I heard back from two. Their questions surprised me. One asked why should we do such a thing, saying this effort was based on fear. The other said weren't we to leave this alone? Maybe this was supposed to happen to them? I couldn't help but wonder, where was their compassion?

I responded:

"The entire east coast? Millions affected? Stand by and do nothing, if it will help in any way? No one needs disaster. If help can be provided, withhold it? Each person will still get whatever they need from this (in spiritual growth).

"p.s. I'm not anywhere near (the middle of the country, nowhere near a coast of any kind). This was not a personal insight but a clairvoyant one. It *came* to me, so shared it; I did not seek it out.

"When one has the ability to help alleviate the magnitude of a major disaster before it arrives, just stand by and do nothing? What about the millions of lives affected in some way? Let them suffer their own fate? Do nothing? That is the polar opposite of everything the Insight has taught me for the last almost forty years, from the Higher Self.

"It's a small task after all, easy to give and let it be whatever it will be (no fret over it. It is merely to help 'balance' the energy if it will help. The energy will do what it will do. That doesn't mean we have to step aside and just take whatever nature dishes out.

"Besides, what about those people who do want help? This is a short easy tool for anyone to know how to use in their own personal lives. (As I was previously 'given' on numerous occasions, during immediate personal situations ... and it 'came' to me ... and it worked. So I have learned that when the Insight is given, listen, because there is always a reason, even if we don't know what it is.)"

Calming Strong Winds

and the Hurricane

3/27/12:

Katie to ME: "We've had significant wings [Wyoming]. Last night was kinda scary—dark clouds, whistling wind, etc. I was pretty nervous. So I decided to use what I read in the workbook [*Intuition for Every Day*] about calling forth help and redirecting the weather. I held my hands up (which I immediately felt get warm) and invoked the universe to shield our home and property. I saw [envisioned] a bubble around us and it glowed blue. I asked for help from the angels and it only took a couple of minutes, and then like you said in the book—you just let it go and knew it would be okay. While I was in the process of doing this, I could hear the wind diminishing and when I went back in the living room—it literally had stopped! My hands get warm when I do reiki, but I don't usually feel it, the person receiving it does. So that was really neat. I just had to share!!"

ME: "Of course they did... You are powerful (a shaman) (intuitive 'knowing')."

Katie: "I just got an email from FEMA about fire down there [Colorado]. I'm sending energy there, too. Oh, and I was one of those that sent energy to that hurricane on the east coast [2011]—so many family members live there. I remember telling my mom that a bunch of us were sending energy to dissipate it before it got there.... I don't know that she believed me, but I know we had an effect!"

ME: "I know we did, too. It was the only time I felt 'prompted' to do something like that... I'm sure it made a difference (intuitive 'knowing')."

Katie: "Goosebumps on the shaman comment. I'm studying shamanism!"

ME: "Oh, wow.... Ha ha ha. I must have 'gotten' that as an affirmation for you. You do know that all this 'intuitive" channeled' stuff is merely tapping into the consciousness.... plugging into you, your whole self. Ancient Woman. Yes, we live in an era when [personal shamanism] will be needed more and more."

It has occurred to me that all of these *prevented* weather events were air-driven. Whether tornado, hurricane, or flash flood, they were all moved by the *currents.* So that, affecting these climate events came down to one simple method: redirecting the *flow* of the currents.

How to Be Safe No Matter Where You Are

Heed your inner warning. When it comes upon you, respond quickly. If you feel a sense of danger, take immediate precaution. You may not know why. You may not know the full answer. Nevertheless, acknowledge the fear that fully embraces you and accordingly protect yourself, your loved ones, and your circumstances.

To command nature in the midst of an impending disaster, intuitively and knowingly decree: "Be gone!"

Quickly pull in a cushion of light around you and around all that you set visually within your mind's eye. Describe in that instant all that you perceive as potential danger and *command* it away.

The life force in us—generally felt as tingling, vibrating, chills, shivers, or radiating heat—is just as real as electricity and just as potent. When properly focused—as a shield of impenetrable energy visualized around you as a brilliant white light—this life force magnificently can deter such effects as floods, tornadoes, and physical harm from other persons or circumstances.

When attuned to your inner radar, you are able to perceive danger as it approaches and sense what lies ahead; to feel and decipher intuitively the *inner resonance* warning you about potential harm to you, your loved ones, pets, home, belongings, and other people.

By relinquishing the desire to completely control your life, you can enable yourself to rely on the inner power to guide you—which is an effective tool of warning *before* you may have any concrete knowledge of something that is about to happen.

If you feel an inner signal of impending danger, alter your actions immediately. Quickly pull in a vortex of light around you. *Command* the universe to shield you. Ask the angels for guidance and safekeeping. Then be still *within*.

The Divine Mind says:

> *"When you are disciplined in the use of the power and of the light, nothing in life can harm you."*

With an attuned and heightened perception, we are able to endure potential hazards; in some cases, even forestall an environmental impact, keep danger away or prevent a disaster, at least to our own environment. You can protect yourself by using the focused power of your mind *and* the natural laws of life. Pull in your innate powerful and extraordinary ability to facilitate an energy shield around you.

When you know unequivocally that you are self-empowered, you can pull in and exactly apply the powerful and innate laws of life—at any time you need them, in their full array—even though in your normal state you may not understand why or how it works.

Mind creates. Mind communicates. Mental energy directed with a clear and sure *intention* is able to alter even the forces of nature.

PROTECTING A LOVED ONE

How I Brought My Lost Dog Back To Me — Five Times!

Using the same innate power and Protection Ritual, I averted potential harm during numerous other kinds of situations, including several potential automobile accidents and threatening persons.

This power also works to find lost pets. I brought Cabra, my timid and naive miniature schnauzer, home safely—and promptly—five times over the years. I also shared this "Finding Your Lost Pet Technique" with twelve other people who also retrieved their lost pets, except in one instance where the animal had already died.

The first time, Cabra was three months old and had been with me only a month. It was three a.m. and she had to go outside. I threw on slippers and my full-length terry-cloth robe and took her out into a blinding rain in the pitch dark night.

Somehow Cabra got away from me; I didn't know there was a hole in the fence of our little side yard. I panicked and began calling for Cabra and searched the entire block for over an hour.

At last, standing in the middle of the little yard in the dark rain, and crying, I gave up.

Just then mental images and *knowing* began flowing into my mind like a procedure to follow. I *saw* Cabra surrounded by a protecting white light and angels around her. I saw her in my arms and holding her to my heart. I saw a cord of white light between her heart and mine, showing our connection and revealing that she was alive.

I then spoke aloud the affirmations that were coming into my mind, calling on all the angels to watch over Cabra and keep her safe, especially Archangel Michael. I then turned Cabra's life over to the Universe and released her, praying that she would return—unharmed, quickly and safely. Then I let her go.

In *that* instant, in the dark heavy night rain, I heard a whimper behind me and I turned. My floppy-eared puppy was standing drenched and bedraggled at my feet. *Goodness!* I fell to my knees and swept her up in my arms, weeping. *Oh, my God. It was real. It really worked.* I was stunned ... and grateful.

I never forgot the ritual after that. I used it four more times with Cabra and in many other instances where I felt danger.

The second time Cabra got lost, she was six months old. We were walking in a large joggers park in Colorado Springs early one weekday morning. I was talking with my woman friend, Jan, and not paying close attention to Cabra. I didn't have Cabra on her leash because she was still a puppy and she behaved well. Suddenly I realized she wasn't around me. I couldn't see her. I panicked.

Jan helped me search the park for over an hour, but to no avail. At last, Jan had to leave for work (I was no longer at the job; I was freelancing by now, doing intuitive readings). In great distress, I dropped onto a park bench. It was then I recalled the Protection Ritual I had been *given* the first time Cabra was lost.

I paused, closed my eyes, sat up ramrod straight, with my feet flat on the ground and my hands in receptive mode, with palms up and each thumb and forefinger touching. The Ritual *came* to me again, just as before, and I visualized the protection. Once again I saw Cabra in my arms and the cord of light between our hearts. Once again I saw a protecting light around her. Once again I asked the angels to keep Cabra safe and unharmed and, if possible, return her to me.

Then a *calm* settled over me and I *knew* I had done all I could and could do no more ... and I actually felt totally at peace. I released the outcome to the Universe and drove home the forty minutes distance by car. As soon as I arrived home, a phone message was flashing on my answering machine. Someone had found Cabra! I immediately drove back downtown to pick her up. She had crossed a major busy downtown intersection during morning rush hour and she was unharmed!

The third time Cabra got lost, we were hiking in a wilderness area at Bear Creek Canyon near Cheyenne Mountain. Cabra was two years old. As usual here, I let her off the leash so she could run free, because I enjoyed watching her scamper and explore and dash around in big circles. Again, I wasn't watching her closely and she wandered off and didn't respond to my calls. (I learned later that she was hard of hearing.)

After searching for three hours, until dark, in great despair I plopped onto the earth and at last turned my mind and heart over to the Protection Ritual, not knowing what else to do. When the ritual was *finished,* the *peace* settled over me ... as before. I then knew it was done, that I had done all I could and could do no more. Again, I truly released the outcome to the Universe and went home.

Just after I arrived home, the phone rang. Someone had picked up Cabra on the trail (during the time when I was sending her the protection). I immediately went back to pick Cabra up. I was so relieved! Once again, the angels had brought my little angel back home to me! Again, safe and unharmed.

The fourth incident was pretty much the same, but I don't recall the details. The fifth and last time Cabra got lost, she was old, fourteen. She had arthritis, she was losing her eyesight, and her hearing was very poor, but she still loved to explore and wander and she still had her sense of smell. I was living in a one-level four-plex in south Denver where we four tenants shared a single fenced backyard (third home after living with Ray in Northglenn). I often left Cabra in the yard to play on her own on nice sunny days (of which there are many in Denver, Colorado) and chase squirrels along the fence. Someone had left the gate open!

Cabra, a gentle innocent soul, had wandered out of the yard and was gone at least a half hour before I realized it. We lived just off University Boulevard, a major street that was always rushing with four lanes of traffic. I raced around on foot, crossing the streets in all directions, calling Cabra. I couldn't find her! Then I got in my car and drove around, widening my search for several blocks in every direction.

After searching futilely for several hours, I finally went home. I plopped into my ragged old recliner and cried. *Then* I remembered to turn my mind and heart over to the Protection Ritual. After completing the ritual, once again I *knew* I had done all I had could and could do no more.

Then the idea *occurred* to me to call the Dumb Friends League (not the animal shelters) and notify them that my dog was lost—just in case, even though Cabra wasn't wearing her collar or ID tag (because I hadn't expected her to be out of the yard, and I didn't like making her wear it otherwise).

This was a desperate evening for me. Although I felt the same peace as I always had before, I realized this could be Cabra's way of "checking out" of her body, dying. She was old and ill. Although I hadn't felt it was quite her time to go, I thought maybe she was ready ... so in my heart I released her. I cried at the thought, but I released her ... and thanked her for spending her life with me these many years, the sweet little soul.

The Indian Summer weather was mild and pleasant for now, however a major snow blizzard was forecast for tonight. I worried more for Cabra's suffering than her possible death or my loss of her in my life.

It snowed heavily all night, six inches, very unusual for Denver (not in the mountains, but in the foothills east of the Rockies). When Cabra had wandered off, the weather was still warm and calm. By nightfall, the blizzard was well underway. The blustering wind rattled the windows. I worried desperately for Cabra, but didn't know what else I could do. I *knew* the Ritual was the greatest gift I could give her. I had to trust ... and allow ... whatever might come.

Come morning, I received a phone call. A lady who lived six blocks away, across the busy boulevard, had found Cabra the night before—before the snowfall—and had taken her in. Cabra had been wandering through the alley, sniffing her way. The lady had cared for Cabra overnight, then the next morning called the Dumb Friends

League (not the animal shelters) and they gave her my phone number. Without an ID tag, the only way the connection was made was by my description of Cabra: an old shaggy miniature schnauzer with floppy ears and a very sweet, gentle disposition. In fact, the lady had decided to keep Cabra if she couldn't find the owner. Fortunately for me, Cabra came home—*once again!* I was so grateful ... to Cabra for not leaving me yet, and to the angels for once again bringing her back to me.

The Protection Ritual given to me *from the angels* has worked every time I have used it. The secret is in letting go.

First, I visualize. Then I affirm. When the calmness—the peace—washes over me, I let go. I truly release the outcome to the highest good. As soon as I let go, what I ask for happens—as if by magic, yet it is natural law.

CLEARING NEGATIVE THOUGHT FORMS

When you sense or feel as if a dark cloud is hanging over you, it is probably a *thought form* rather than a being. It may be your own negative thoughts (most likely), or you may have picked it up from people around you, or both.

- Visualize a column of light straight up through your body, through the top of your head, connecting you to your Higher Self. Hold the image while focusing on something like nature, such as mountains, to *ground* your energy.

- To release, break up, and dissipate the *thought form:* Shout! Yell! A good place to do this is in your car (alone) on the freeway, while driving up a mountain pass, while driving alongside the ocean, somewhere isolated, with the windows rolled up—so you can truly let go!

The Power disintegrates all lower energies and vibrations (which affect mental, emotional, and physical). Be commanding! Invoke your power! Embolden your *inner fire ...* your true Self. Feel your core ... your strength! Continue until you feel *connected!*

That Someone At Work

Once on a new job (the one right after my cosmic awakening), the supervisor seemed to have it out for me all the time and I hated going to work because she was always on my case. The job was very unpleasant and every day after I arrived, I got severe stomach cramps. I got to where I did whatever I could to avoid her.

One day it *occurred* to me (the way angels give me guidance) to visualize *pink* light around the woman every time I saw her or thought about her. So, I did.

In only a few days, her attitude toward me shifted and she became friendly and even befriended herself to me. It was a complete turnabout. I was amazed. This exercise proved to me how powerful visualization is and how truly effective our thoughts and attitudes are.

INNER SEEING

THE MIND'S EYE

Humans are inherently and naturally intuitive, and inner vision is just as natural as breathing. Being able to see-perceive-sense is an *inborn survival instinct* that has always been with us. As we have become more intellectual as a species, we have more and more denied the innate sensory mechanisms that are a part of our physical heritage.

In this chapter, I describe my observations during clairvoyant intuitive soul readings, in case this helps you to better understand images that may come to *you.* The symbolisms I give here are mainly for your awareness of what is possible. My suggestion is merely to follow whatever images do appear in your own mind's eye and see what they do. Watch them and observe. Also, remember, they are often humorous.

Then trust your sense of what meanings the images are trying to convey (your intuition). Consider a wide spectrum and a broad range of possibilities. The mind is vast, and interpretations are not narrow or limited to a single point of view or way of comprehending. Look at all of it. Observe. Watch. Feel. Sense. Intuit. Listen.

I began to realize my own intuitive senses at the age of thirty. I didn't train with anyone. This was a latent ability that was dormant until my spontaneous spiritual awakening in November 1975.

Later, during an exceptionally deep meditation, I found myself entering (alone) a verbal dialogue—out loud—with my Oversoul. I was shown the very clear outline of my life plan, the blueprint of what I had decided before birth that I wanted to accomplish in this life. I now viewed this contract I had signed, in the etheric plane, for fulfilling my heart's vision.

Intuitive abilities (including spiritual insight, discernment, innate knowing, and warrior empowerment) are only a part of my gifts.

The clairvoyant soul readings I have done since 1977 have honed my perceptions to an ever finer degree; especially, the mini readings at street festivals and metaphysical fairs, when readings follow one after another, hour after hour, day after day. This intense activity revealed many new insights to me about the inner vision and also enhanced my clairvoyant abilities.

When I get mental pictures while reading an individual, I realize that I am drawing on a multi-layer of several different sources at the same time. Immediately, I simultaneously perceive an influx of multiple images, impressions, feelings, and ideas. I sort these out *intuitively,* through sensing and empathic feeling. I don't try to think it through, nor discern intellectually. I certainly do not deny, discount, or censor any of the information. It is what it is.

In the Zone, I allow my *knowing* Self to guide the process and reveal the details (which I see, hear, feel, and just know). I am then able to pull these into a sharper focus. It's all there (it's always with us and around us). The task is merely honing in, zeroing in, focusing in— ZONING IN—mentally on a *detail* and allowing your whole being to sense–perceive–comprehend what is there before you and around you.

Human beings think in pictures (dreams, visions, daydreams). We even talk in metaphors. When I am reading for someone, it is the sitter's task to understand whether the image conveyed is a symbolic metaphor or a literal representation. Often I do *know* if it is symbolic. It is less possible to identify an actual truth, although this is frequently confirmed.

CLAIRVOYANT SYMBOLS

Some examples of literal images I have seen in clairvoyant readings have been confirmed. For example, in my mind's eye I saw graduation caps being tossed into the air. At the very least this picture meant to me that the person would be well-advised to attend college. This symbol expressed to me (through felt-knowing) exuberance and a very positive energy and success at reaching a goal, possibly related to higher education. With such a symbol, there can be many nuances of meaning and interpretation for both the present and future. In this instance, the individual had just graduated from college yesterday, so *this* symbolism, while typical of the kinds of imagery that show up in a reading, was verified as already true. Such validation added credibility to the other unknown future facts given in the reading.

Another example: I perceived the man I was reading climbing to a high point of elevation. I also felt a sense of him flying. At the same time, I saw mathematical symbols floating in the air over and around his head, and I could imagine him constructing mechanical or engineering types of components. Then I saw a plane getting off the ground. My empathic and intuitive deduction perceived that he might be gifted as an aerospace engineer, whether or not he was aware of this talent or utilizing it. In fact, he was, which he informed me after the reading. He was an aerospace engineer.

Three additional examples: I saw an arc of many nations' flags. After the reading, the young girl informed me that she was planning to study international law. In another reading on the same day, for a middle-aged woman (also an intuitive reader), when she asked about her ten-year-old daughter, I saw the girl playing a violin; the woman afterwards told me that her daughter had been wanting a violin and was very interested in music. I also had a picture of this same woman signing a legal document, such as a contract, in the near future. She said I was the third person to *see* this for her recently. although as yet she didn't know what it was about.

I always wonder how on earth this works. I am as amazed and in awe of these capabilities of the higher mind as anyone else. I also sense and know intuitively that this talent is something any human being can do when properly focused (felt within, you know when you are there).

I sense that this ability is more than just guessing. Although many people are very astute and consciously able to discern and glean information about others, this has never been an ability I could intentionally muster. That would be too much effort. Yet when I put myself into an altered state of mind, which I *feel–sense–perceive–know* when I am there, it just comes. The information is just there.

I have come to realize that it is always there for anyone to pick up on. It's as if images, pictures, thoughts, and emotions are always floating around us and through us, and someone else is able to see them, feel them, hear them, know them. It's like we are all walking around with these pictures and images projecting from our minds and bodies. We are indeed walking virtual realities, available to anyone willing to take a moment to slow down and observe.

I do believe we are all capable of slowing down our perceptions to a degree that we can consciously look at the subtle nonphysical images, feel the subtle nonphysical impressions, and hear the subtle nonphysical thoughts floating around in the air all the time. I do believe we are always *reacting* to these, although usually unconsciously. It's more a matter of learning to trust and accept what we sense and perceive is another person's thought, feeling, or desire than whether it is real or not. We all do it. We just don't trust what we know.

The goal, therefore, is learning to trust our senses, and that trust comes with practice. It's not so much whether it's real or even if it's there. It's more a matter of just experiencing and assuming it is true ... unless or until otherwise proven.

Also, before giving a clairvoyant reading, I have always doubted ("stage fright"), feeling this couldn't possibly be real—until I am in the

ZONE. Time and again—every time (14,000+ times)—it has been verified (by the person's reactions and responses) that this ability, this gift, is indeed real, in fact shockingly so to most of the people who've had a reading. That's just incredible. We human beings are truly amazing.

When I am in The Zone, I *know* the information is true (or at least the gist of what is being conveyed is true). I can feel it. When I am not there, I feel just as human as everyone else.

Such information comes from the natural Self (the sitter's Higher Self and mine). We are all a part of a vast ocean of energy, which is consciousness itself. This consciousness is what we call vibration, which takes many forms. It is our nature—as human beings—to exude this vibration of the Eternal Oneness. This vibration is an *energy force.* As an evolving point of consciousness of the All, which each of us is, we are continuously striving to express and experience and become the *wholeness.*

It is very difficult to define in words the fluidity of images and ideas that flash through my mind during a clairvoyant reading. In the following passages, I have tried to grasp some of the metaphors and symbolisms that have been especially striking and noteworthy. What is very clear is that any picture presents the recipient with volumes of information and nuances of meaning that can be interpreted only intuitively, then must be experienced in real life one day at a time. While there is no real way of knowing how accurate the details are in the following visual metaphors and symbolic images, they feel total when I am there. About ninety-eight percent has been validated by the sitters themselves.

Psychic interpretation is to a great degree personal and dependent on the perceiver's life experiences and beliefs. I share the following examples in case there are any parallels that may be useful to you. It is possible that these metaphors are more than my personal comprehension and may be archetypes, at least in our Western culture. Hopefully, you will find some use for these images and they will convey possibilities to what your own imagination can see and what possible interpretations they might have for you. You might find these mental translations similar to dream symbols, yet I feel they are more. Also keep in mind, these are only a few of countless possible categories; and, within each category, only a few of countless possible images are listed.

- Hearts, roses, energy intertwined, walls, barriers, domes, golden ring on/off/falling off/staying on a wedding finger, heart throbbing: *romance, relationship, true love, soul mate, life mate, life partner.* (Questions that might be asked: This one? Someone else? How many? When? Where?)

- Mountains, stairs, climbing, heights: *seeing, far seeing, knowing, success, reaching goal.* (Questions to glean more information: Life path? Business? Career? Spiritual?)

- Planes, travel. (Questions: Literal or symbolic?)

- A female in full pregnancy form: *reveals someone being pregnant, probably means soon.*

- A door frame with many marks of measuring the height of a child: *shows growth, maturity, through life, beyond this moment.*

- Heaven pouring out money or gold or a river: *financial flow.*

- Many paths: *resources, sources, opportunities, choices, options.*

- People coming toward you: *support, assistance, partners, associates, helpers.*

- Thundercloud overhead, with rain: *trouble, challenges, how to deal with and overcome.*

- Lightning bolts striking, apparently haphazardly: *conflict, danger, to be aware/prepare/observe.*

- Light or dark: *reflects situation/energy.*

- On a stage or podium, performing or speaking: *potential, talent, public, form of expression.*

- Bent over feverishly writing, volumes of books: *a writer, something to be written.*

- Juggling: *life activities, difficult or managing and to what degree.*

- Past lives: *overlapping, symbol for current life; mirrors continuing infinitely, relationships, lessons being learned, talents of this life.*

- Crown of stars: *highly evolved spiritually, wisdom.*

- Antahkarana: *line of light/link to Higher Self, open to spiritual plane, receptive to Spirit.*

- A being leaning over and speaking to you through the line of light: *you are able to channel Spirit.*

- Angels around: *protection, guidance, support, direction.*

- A plain of dim light, or light, with spirit forms walking about or moving in it: *spirit world.*

- You are wondering about several people sharing a venture or business. Suppose the plan is three people. In one reading, as soon as the woman mentioned this, I saw one person fall away "out of the picture" and two remain, and that the two were sufficient. This indicated that one of the potential partners would not remain or probably would choose not to participate.

Past—Present—Future

When I am visualizing for a person, in my mind's eye, his or her life plane is a large flat horizon stretching out before me left to right as far as my 360° peripheral vision (I see behind me, too). None of the following would be absolute truth in every instance but serve as a general guide. Your own senses will tell you whether a perception you have matches this guide or is a variable (which is always possible).

- Images, events, scenarios *straight ahead* that scope across the plane both left and right: generally the *future,* such as several paths that appear (choices) or doors (opportunities).

- A path *straight before you* (your life path, the path you are on).

- Images *alongside* the path (reveal how things are going, now and soon ahead).

- Images of *other people* along your path, or approaching you (tell you whether you are or will do something alone or as part of a group, or with a partner such as in business or a venture).

- *Behind you* (may not be visible, but felt—"baggage" you are carrying from your past, an extraordinary burden holding you back which you need to release/let go in order to move forward in your life and feel free).

- Coming from or on *the right* (the *future*).

- Coming from *the left* (the *past*).

Example of an image from the past: I recently had the mental image of a person lying flat as if deceased; in my mental picture, on the left of the path before me. I said to the middle-aged woman, "I may have something sad to say. Do you want to hear it?" She answered, "Yes." I then said, "I think someone is about to die. It feels maternal, like a mother, and feels soon in time." The woman said her mother had just died a month before. I wondered why I would receive such an image. I immediately knew it was because someone in the sitter's life would soon become pregnant and the new child would be the woman's deceased mother who felt she had unfinished business in the world. This made sense to the sitter. We were then both able to glean much useful information about the new child's personality and character, why the soul (the mother) was returning, how she could be recognized, and how to help her and relate to her in her new life. Until this reading, I hadn't yet realized that *left* of the path in an imagery represented the past. Now it was clear to me. Every reading has taught me something more about how the Mind works and how our energies communicate who we are.

Staircase to Heaven

I have had a few people ask about someone they expected to die. For such a question, I look for a picture rather than just verbally channel a response, because pictures are self-explanatory and do not necessarily require my interpretation. In all such cases, I have seen a wide staircase from here into Heaven and angels floating up and down as if traveling regularly to Earth and back. In the first instance that this happened, the person seen being taken to Heaven up the staircase did pass over soon after the reading (within two months).

I wondered why such information would be received. One, it was requested. Two, the picture conveyed comfort, to inform the sitter of the whole picture of that soul's process and the development of that relative or friend passing over. Such information serves a healing purpose for the sitter and for no other reason is given. It gives the person remaining in life a greater comprehension of the whole experience of life and death and the transition to what comes after this world. Such a reading gives peace.

Time

Activity on the distant horizon in a reading seems to indicate more distance in *time*. A figure moving in *this* direction indicates the speed or hesitancy of an activity or relationship approaching the sitter's present life. On the doorstep or knocking at the door feels imminent.

A timeline is variable, however, because Spirit seems to have its own agenda for *when* things actually will occur. Nevertheless, such imagery can give you a gauge of whether a timeline will be sooner rather than later or a long time in the future (weeks, months, years). It's something to go by at least. Waiting is the hardest part of being human, especially when your intuition tells you something will for sure happen. *But when?*

Psyching Information

Ultimately, first assume that your own images are symbolic, revealing to you whatever you need to know about yourself and your life. If you also happen to identify that they are literal, so much the better for the confirmation. At the very least, images reveal possible choices, options, and directions in life that will bring you the most fulfillment—for which you were born.

No matter what images might arise in your awareness—such as during meditation, on waking in the morning, an insight that flashes to you during the day, or a dream—such insights merely point the way to go *in the moment.* Truly, we are guided continuously. No piece of information is a final, absolute, unchangeable truth. Our lives are fluid ... because our needs, feelings, thoughts, choices, and circumstances are always changing. Therefore, it is essential to always be attuned to what you are sensing *right now.* That, in fact, is all any of us has to go by: *this* moment, this *feeling,* this inner *knowing.*

With metaphors like those given above, I do not consciously choose or decide any symbol or picture. The first instance of their appearance to me reveals what they represent (through my consciousness) for the individual or myself. For me, understanding always has *followed* an event, from the very beginning of my psychic opening in 1975.

I have observed that while doing a reading, I often intuitively (unconsciously) rub my forehead. It's almost as if this is stimulating the ability to retrieve the information. Perhaps it is stimulating the pituitary gland. I have observed that this function seems to derive *seeing* images and perceiving interpretations.

Likewise, sometimes I automatically place one or both hands over my heart while reading a person. This seems indicative of an especially strong empathic connection with that person or something being *received* for that individual. Or it can relate to someone the person is asking about. This must have to do with stimulating, or connecting to, a source center for empathy.

Most distinctly, I have learned that *breath* is the single most important factor in reaching an altered state, psyching information, and channeling materials, as for a book. Often, at the beginning of doing a clairvoyant reading, especially during a psychic fair, I find myself automatically expelling breaths, as if clearing to a receptive space. With this often come extremely deep short breaths similar to yawns. The body seems to know what it needs to do for the mind and energy to reach a certain attunement and receptivity at a psychic level (beyond ordinary attention).

During readings, I also frequently expel breaths in-between phases or cycles of information, such as pertaining to individual areas of focus or intention. At the same time, I also continuously automatically breathe deeply, to draw in a fresh mental and psychic state of mind. None of this is planned or consciously chosen or determined.

I also often expel breaths at the end of readings, especially during psychic fairs where I sometimes get up and move around to shake off the energies.

What is important is at the end of the day to take a shower and cleanse both the body and mind as well as the aura field.

When coming into FOCUS, I feel a very directed alignment of energy pulling into my center both physically and mentally. It reminds me of experiencing Tai Chi movements, wherein the breath aligns with body postures and gestures and the mind ZEROS IN with a laser intention. Part of this instinctive posturing by the body is touching the thumb and forefinger on each hand, as if they are the poles of a battery charge. All of this pulls me into THE ZONE. I have learned that the best approach is just to *feel* the energy and follow my body's natural instincts.

When I am deep in the focus, I remain fully aware and alert. I am merely allowing myself to go to a more subtle place in my being. My eyelids usually flutter, as during sleep or self-hypnosis. This is a good indicator of having reached LEVEL. I myself always remain fully conscious. I used to wish I could be a trance channel. Now I realize that being a conscious channel is a great advantage, because I get to experience and remember everything and, should I desire to, I can stop anytime I want (though I've never needed to or wanted to).

Being in the ZONE or at LEVEL is a subtle sense of *focused intention* and *contained fervor.* It is not casual or frivolous. Physical sensations are present and are cues that I am not in my usual active state.

Reaching this within self is the result of focusing our whole being and reminds me of the strict adherence one must feel when practicing a martial art. There is an extraordinary sensitivity and the entire body and mind become like a musical instrument.

The Preparation

Before doing a reading for a person, or to attune prior to a day's event such as a psychic fair, my preparation includes: deep breathing, the white light, calling in protection and alignment.

After a meditation to take me to LEVEL, I then ask the angels to be with me and around me, to speak for me and through me *for the highest good of all.*

I visualize my light as a column of energy moving straight up and connecting me with my soul and the I AM (God, the Divine).

I also see all others I will meet today surrounded by their angels and connected to their souls and the I AM.

Then I see each individual standing before me and us connected by light between all of our chakras, Higher Selves, and the I AM—only for the time we will be together, then it will dissolve.

I release myself to the voice of their souls and their angels during this time, that their thoughts will be my thoughts, their needs my needs, and their consciousness my consciousness. In this way, I am able to be *present* for them and connect into their vibration and Higher Self awareness. This enables me to provide essential insights into their whole Selves as well as their everyday lives.

Then it is over. It is finished. The responsibility then lies with the individual to use the insights in the best way possible, to trust their own inner *knowing* on a day-to-day basis ... because that is what we all have to do.

For all the insights someone else may be able to glean for us, we ourselves have to live it. We make the choices ... by learning to trust our instincts and acting upon them.

READING YOURSELF

Ball of Light, Line of Light, Pointing the Way

The *easiest visual tool* for reading yourself is watching the white light, the energy, the life force in your mind's eye. In the privacy of your personal sanctuary (alone) look for a ball of light, an energy ball. Watch the energy. See what it does. Does it glow and expand? Or shrink and dim? That's your answer.

Where

If you're wondering about a place, like where to move—in your mind's eye look at a map. Start with the ball of energy where you live now (the city). Watch the energy. Does it move? Is there a line of light? Which direction does it go? Up (north), down (south), left (west), right (east), diagonal? Follow the line of light to the new ball of energy. Look where the light *settles* on the map. Wherever that is, you owe it to yourself to check the place out and see how it *feels.*

If you are confirming whether to go to a certain place or stay where you are, *follow the energy.* The place to be is where the energy *settles* and is strongest and brightest—especially if it *pulsates.*

When

If you want to know *when* to do something, in your mind's eye look at a calendar and flip through the months one at a time. Watch the energy. Also *feel* the energy. *When* does it pick up speed? *When* does it stop or reach an end point? You can do this also by the year— through *feeling.* While specific details may change with time, this at least gives you a target date and can guide you on whether to act now or in the near future, or wait for now and recheck later on or when the *knowing* strikes.

What

If you want to know whether to do a particular thing, such as take a particular job or visit a particular place or building, go there first in your mind's eye and look at its energy. Is there expansive light around it? Or is it dark and forbidding? That's your answer.

Who

The same applies to people. If you're wondering whether you can trust a person, or if a person is dangerous—in your mind's eye (in the privacy of your personal sanctuary) look at the energy. You may see colors. You may see smooth vital joyful light, or dark jagged streaks or spots. A line of light from the person's crown straight up into the heavens shows alignment with the spiritual Self. *Ultimately, trust your instincts:* in both visions and in the person's presence.

Basically, when watching the light in your mind's eye, notice how it flows, easy or not, abundantly or not. Feel *where* it goes, or wants you to go—as if it is subtly pulling you to consider a particular direction or idea. It is always worth your time to at least investigate the possibility. You won't know if something can be done or if you want it, unless you follow through.

Reading yourself isn't always easy. But when it does work, it's like magic.

As described above, *the first clue to right action* is: If you feel any inner resistance, doubt or uncertainty, wait, do not act. The uncomfortable nagging is a subtle psychic cue that something is amiss. It may be only about you and nothing to do with the other person. Nevertheless, it is important to acknowledge what is or is not in your personal best interest.

HOW TO MAKE THE RIGHT CHOICE

A week before Thanksgiving 2002, I was considering trading in my ten-year-old Toyota Paseo for a more recent model with a full-service warranty. After evaluating the most likely candidates, by researching the Consumer Reports Used Cars book, I decided that aside from a Toyota Camry or Corolla, the next best candidate financially would be the Geo Prizm. My search in the Yellow Pages for the Geo turned up nothing. I couldn't find it and didn't know where else to look.

The next day my editing business schedule juggled itself around and I found myself with unexpected free time on this Wednesday. Rather than wait a few days to go to KIA for their seven-to-ten year warranty, I decided to go now and see what they had to offer. I had no intention of buying today. I was just beginning the process.

The first car the salesman took me to was a Chevy Prizm (ditto the Geo Prizm!). I was stunned. This had to be an omen, I said to myself. I still believed in omens.

I spent the next two or three hours test-driving the car, twice, and negotiating the deal. I wanted the car. It was new, they offered a seven-year service warranty for practically free (after my negotiation), the sticker price was $3,000 under book value (according to the Consumer Guide). Yet something nagged at me. I would have to put $1,000 down which I hadn't planned on spending (even though I had it, which was rare), I wouldn't get the ninety-day payment deferment, my insurance would increase by one-third, my monthly payments would increase by fifty dollars for an additional four years, and I still owed one year on my current car. Plus, I was offered only $1,500 trade-in and I still owed the finance company $2,300 (the reason for needing the down payment). The low trade-in value was mainly because the hood and front fenders were unpainted new black parts (to go with my otherwise teal blue two-door coupe). I'd had a minor fender-bender just six weeks before and replaced the damaged parts with new sheet metal but not yet painted it. Otherwise, the car was in good condition. Due to its age, however, State Farm "totaled" it, so I elected to keep the car.

State Farm valued the Paseo at $4,000 (with my add-on CD player and security system), less my $2,000 deductible (won't do that again!). They paid me *exactly* the amount I needed to replace the damaged parts, without painting; the professional painting of only those front parts would have been $1,500, so I decided to wait until spring and find a $500 Maaco deal to repaint the entire car—more for my money and less out-of-pocket.

With the low trade-in value at KIA, plus needing to invest $1,000, although I wanted the new Chevy Prizm I just didn't feel ready for that extra expense, because December and January typically had been my slowest income season of the year. Although the finance company was willing to work with me, I felt hesitant—so we didn't deal that day. Meanwhile, the finance officer said he would talk to the bank and see what more favorable terms they could work out.

That afternoon, Thursday, I got a phone call for a big job to format and edit a Ph.D. dissertation. It was a sure deal because of a referral. I felt financial relief and now more certainty about buying the new car. I *could* manage the increased payment. I could even handle the increased insurance. I didn't want to give up a thousand dollars, but at least I had it ... and that was a new pattern.

The expected twenty-four hour wait to hear back from KIA's bank extended into another day. While waiting, to verify the *right course of action* I checked my pendulum for a *yes* or *no* because this technique had proven consistently reliable over the years. On one occasion, I had "cured" myself of a serious intestinal infection (a miscalculated self-colonic treatment) by using the pendulum to determine which vitamins and herbs to use and at what dosages. Curiously, the dosages were extremely high on the first day, then throughout that day and on the subsequent days reduced as my symptoms improved ... until I reached normal in both physical health and pendulum readings. I was impressed. I also implicitly trusted the *I Ching Workbook* by R. L. Wing, which I had long ago learned to read intuitively. Both of these resources gave me favorable indicators on buying a new car.

Interestingly though, despite these two favorable readings on myself, throughout this process—from the beginning, even before I went car shopping—whenever I asked my *inner voice* whether I should buy a new car, the answer consistently was, *Keep your car.* So I had a dilemma. I was too emotionally caught up in this process to objectively know what to do or how to read all the variables, psychic and otherwise. I was also unable to clearly observe a mental energy picture. So what could I do? How could I decide?

Friday I met with the Ph.D. client and received the substantial retainer. Feeling confident, I called the salesman at KIA to confirm that I *did* want the car. I was feeling buoyant. He wanted the sale, too, but was still waiting on an answer from the bank. Something was snagging, I realized. He said we should have a final deal by the next morning, Saturday. *Great!* I thought.

However, when I woke up Saturday, I felt differently. I had a clear *instinct* (finally). The "snag" in getting the deal, combined with my inner *nagging*, had finally prompted me to remember:

> *Whenever there is any inner resistance or uncertainty:*
> *Delay. Do not act.*

Ah. There it was. Finally, the answer: *Not now.* For whatever reason, *wait.*

Now I knew the *right action.* During these days of *waiting,* I had seen a TV commercial of Maaco offering their $500 premier paint job for half price, cheaper than I'd ever seen it. I was already talking to other car dealers who hadn't seen my currently black-and-blue car yet. Getting the entire car repainted, it would look like new. I would get double or triple the trade-in value of the cost to paint it (the whole car for $250, instead of only the front end for $1,500).

So I drove myself to Maaco and signed the Paseo in for a paint job. When I got home, I called the car salesman at KIA and told him I wasn't going to do the deal. I still had the option of going to another car lot.

Yet *now* I remembered that when driving on the freeway yesterday, my Paseo sounded pretty good after all. The engine felt strong and had good pick up for passing. Maybe I would keep it. Or I could still make a better end-of-the-year deal if I wanted to. Meanwhile, I talked to my lender. Based on the financial facts, I decided it *was* best to wait.

When I picked up my shiny new-looking car the next day, I *knew* the answer. I was buoyant! When I saw the glistening teal-blue body in the winter sunshine, I fell in love with my Paseo all over again ... and renamed her: *Beauty!* Something about that color! Shimmering aquatic deep ocean blue. It filled my heart. No way was I letting this car go.

When trying to make an important decision, sometimes it is easy to misread "the signs" or to read into circumstances what appear to be "omens." My *omens* were finding the very car by chance I had decided I wanted, then having a job show up just when I needed the extra money. I could have gone ahead and been happy with a new car—except it would have strained my finances and caused me undue distress for many months. I really didn't need any more stress.

It's very easy to read into circumstances some otherworldly implication, when it is really about *choice.* This was a *choice.*

I realized then that the I Ching and pendulum indicators to get a newer car were based on my true underlying concern of whether I would be able to manage the increased financial obligation. When I got the new client project, that concern was alleviated so the readings were positive.

I then remembered that *emotional fears and desires affect subconscious responses,* which is how the pendulum and I Ching work. The readings were correct; I *did* receive unexpected income just in time.

Life is a tough call sometimes. Our psychic radar is a good gauge, but we also have a mind and a brain and it takes all of these to make the right decision.

When it comes right down to it, life is about the choices we make *and* being sensible. Luck is part of it, or karma. The rest, though, is just plain old hard work. It's not so much about what divine messages we get, or think we're getting, as *what makes the most sense.* The delay in the car deal gave me time to *listen* to my uncertainty about spending big on a newer car. I had *time* to remember to pay attention to my emotional inner resistance and hesitancy. If it had been absolutely right to buy the new car, I wouldn't have hesitated. I would have known.

There are many ways to read a situation in order to determine the best course of action. However, most important is to feel *absolutely sure.* A decision should not be based on emotional desire but, rather, on a reasoned and balanced evaluation of *all* elements involved.

I've learned that I'd better take a *reasoned* approach on major decisions, because I have a tendency to see *magic* in every opportune circumstance. Message: *Live in the present. Stop living in a dream. Keep my feet on the ground.* No more waiting with baited breath for the magic to free me from the doldrums of life.

Life is about reasoned and balanced choices. Not going off the deep end. We must keep our heads. Sometimes we are blessed by opportune circumstances. Sometimes we are not. The gist is just *live.* Do your best. Be your best. That's all anyone can do.

The answer when making an important decision is not what omens show up, but what is the most practical and commonsense action. Messages from heaven should never take the place of our own valued judgment and overall evaluation of options. The bigger picture and the bottom line are still up to us.

The universe works with us. All we have to do is listen. When you can hear the guidance (in whatever form), it certainly can allay your worries and help you more quickly process and decide on a course of action. I always feel better when I clearly *hear* the guidance. Then I am able to relax and trust that my choice is the right one. It sure has made life easier.

Part II

Honing Your Intuition

TUNING IN: THE BASICS

It is especially beneficial if you do the following beginner exercises sequentially, one after the other. Of course, if you prefer, you may choose to do any one, in any order. Always follow your *feeling—* what *feels* like the right thing to do ... in the moment.

Discovering Your Energy Field

Place your palms around a cup of hot tea. Visualize the tea as pure energy. See it as a bright white light.

- As you sip the tea, visualize this light flowing into you as pure healing energy, and say:

    I cleanse myself of all impurities, doubts, and negative feelings.

    I am pure and whole.

    I allow nothing within me but good, beauty, and love.

- As you drink in the energy: feel revitalized, attuned and ready to receive enlightenment.

- Now set down the cup. Put your hands before you. Briskly rub them until they become warm. Then separate them about six inches, with your palms facing.

- In your mind's eye, visualize the same white light energy. Imagine that energy emanating from your palms, and visualize it sparking.

- Move your hands back and forth and feel the energy pulling between them (as if you are pulling taffy).

- Move your hands around and feel the energy you are pushing and pulling in the air. The energy is almost palpable. This is your energy field, your aura.

Energizing for the Day

Clasp your palms together before you. Visualize a white light energy flowing throughout your body.

- See the energy moving through you as a great pure light of love and peace. You are re-energizing yourself, filling with a new and vibrant vitality.

- Now see this white light expanding, glowing outward from your body and surrounding you as a protective shield. This bubble of white light is your protection against all negative thoughts and actions. It cleanses you and fills you with love and peace toward all and helps you act in a spirit of true oneness.

- Visualize a band of gold around the bubble of white light. This band of gold doubly strengthens the protective bubble of light.

- Keep this light around you at all times.

You can also place this white light around your home, car, office, pets, loved ones, and friends. You can project the light onto negative people and situations (pink works good, too, as with my job supervisor). When you do this, visualize the light around them and see it as a light of loving kindness.

You will find that such a practice actually causes most people to react toward you in a more kindly and thoughtful manner. Situations also turn more in your favor—as long as you are fair and impartial. When you project light and love, you receive it.

Setting Your Focus for the Day

As you go into the following short meditation, set your intention for the day. Imagine the day unfolding. Imagine a different experience. Return to the tender feelings of your innocence. Then give thanks to the Divine.

- Breathe out completely until you fully empty your lungs.

- Now breathe evenly and smoothly for a few minutes, rhythmic breathing: inhaling, holding your breath, then exhaling. Each to the count of eight (or whatever is comfortable for you).

- While doing the rhythmic breathing, be *thinking* the following statements *into* your subconscious mind. Don't worry about the exact procedure. Get into a rhythm and flow.

Inhaling, Holding Your Breath, and Exhaling:

Morning

I command my subconscious and conscious minds to work in harmony with my higher mind throughout this day. I am soulfully aware.

Evening

I see and hear clearly.
I understand and accept fully.
I am my soul on earth.

Practice these affirmations until you are so familiar with them that you can close your eyes and do them from memory. Once you can make these statements easily and smoothly, while rhythmically breathing *add* the following visualization:

- Visualize a tide of golden energy rising through you from the soles of your feet, up through your spine, through the top of your head, and spraying upward and outward like a fountain.

- Imagine your body fully vitalized by this golden fountain of energy. Imagine the golden energy healing you inside and out, energizing your body and mind, and soothing your emotions.

- Once again, see the golden fountain of energy spreading upward through your feet, to your pelvis, ribs, heart, throat, face, crown, and out through your arms and fingertips. See the golden fountain of energy spreading throughout your entire body, cleansing and renewing you.

Morning Jumpstart

Developing a spiritual consciousness is a process similar to physical growth and is brought about by learning and practicing techniques of light. The purpose is to expand the capacity of the mind so that it becomes able to register instantaneous contact with the divine light. For example, to have electricity in a home, it first has to be wired. This Technique in Light corresponds in a body to the wiring in a house. This technique enables your body to receive—*in a flash*—the divine spark of the eternal life energy.

- When you waken, lie completely relaxed from your toes all the way up through your scalp. Visualize a radiant Being of Light at your feet, with the soles of your feet against the soles of the Being. This contact grounds you for divine power to spark throughout your body. Once you have grounded with the Being of Light, that *light* remains with you for the rest of the day.

- Now send your vision soaring upward to an infinite point of light. That point is the station from which inspiration and revelation can be *flashed* into your mind throughout the day, whenever you choose to focus on it.

- Now visualize a *flashing circle of light* from the right side of your head, forward. Then around through the head of the Being of Light. Then back to the left of your head, completing the circle. You are now energized for the day. Your mind is ready and capable of receiving inspiration.

When doing this powerful morning *jumpstart,* don't let your mind wander. *Flash* the images. This will train your mind to *spark.* Don't linger on any part of the technique. This is a *quickening* process. Do the entire Being of Light Technique so quickly that it takes only a *flashing* moment at the start of your day.

How Do You Love Yourself?

- Carry no burden of the past.

- Transcend the ordinary and look to ways of joy. Seek original concepts of truth.

- Relinquish your hold on others. Release, allow. Be not a tyrant.

- Live consciously. Learn to understand the way you have come and the way you now go.

- Be understanding. Forgive your own errors and transmute your fears. Be open to growing and being whole.

- Understand that you will exist forever.

- Self-mastery is *being* love, which is learned. "As he acts, so will he be." *Upanishads.*

THE SIX PRACTICES

ENHANCING AND SHARPENING YOUR INHERENT INTUITION

1. The Breath — Deep Rhythmic Breathing

2. Protection — White Light

3. Grounding — Centering

4. Clearing — Aura Cleansing

5. Aligning — Chakra Balancing

6. Feeling the Connection — Meditation

These six steps further develop our innate intuition and enhance the feeling of oneness with all of life.

These simple steps require only practice and attention and can be achieved by anyone, because intuition is inborn in every human being. It is a part of our genetic makeup. This essential life component is the key to a smoother and more content life. It is also central to heightened consciousness and higher insight.

Once you have learned these Six Basic Steps, you may modify any of them. You also may record them for your personal use, as they are suggested techniques that have worked for me. *Do what works for you.*

Once you find your rhythm, you may complete this entire process in as little as fifteen minutes, although you may stretch the mood to as long as you like (e.g., an hour). The deeper you go into this state, the more satisfaction you will feel.

Daily repetition brings the best results because it trains your subconscious mind to accept a new self-image and belief structure about how to live a full and happy life.

THE BREATH

Awareness Enhancement Practice 1

Deep Rhythmic Breathing

To reach the deep inner silence

Deep rhythmic breathing is the first key to higher conscious awareness.

This is an easy tool for quickly moving into calmness and a deeper level of awareness. Deep breathing alters brainwave patterns and brings in a clearer concentration.[2] Rhythmic belly breathing is so effective that, once mastered, you can use it anywhere, at any time, to quickly reach a deep calm and clear thinking (such as for an exam or a job interview).

Begin by sitting in a comfortable position, in a chair or on the floor, with your back straight, legs and arms uncrossed; or in a yogi position. Leave your eyes barely open for reading this while you shift into the inner silence.

Read slowly and gracefully, to deeply experience every phase of this guided meditation.

If necessary, you can return to full waking consciousness at any time, simply by lifting the index finger of your left hand ... or you may drift now into a meditation ... or you may fall into a natural deep sleep and remain perfectly safe and protected.

---

2 For me, even just this step immediately takes my mind to clarity and writing. So easy.

- Be still, shutting out all distractions. Begin taking several long deep breaths through your nose. Inhale from the depths of your diaphragm (belly breaths).

- Breath slowly, evenly and deeply. Feel your body slowing down, relaxing. Your body is relaxing.

- Visualize air rising slowly, filling your lungs. Inhale *slowly* ... until you can inhale no more.

- Hold for a few seconds. Then exhale slowly through your mouth. Allow every breath to leave your body, until there is no breath left.

- Continue deep breathing, knowing that each breath is taking you deeper and deeper into consciousness.

- As you drift deeper into this relaxed state of full awareness, you may begin to feel lightheaded. Feel a wave of warm relaxation flowing throughout your body. You are feeling totally relaxed and at ease.

- The relaxing power is moving up through your feet, calves, thighs, legs, relaxing your legs. Warm, relaxing power. Warm, relaxing power.

- This relaxing power comes into the fingers of your hands, relaxing your hands, relaxing your forearms, relaxing your upper arms, relaxing.

- This relaxing power is flowing upward through your spine, through all the organs of your body, relaxing your body, relaxing your stomach muscles, relaxing all the muscles of your back.

- This relaxing power is moving up through your shoulders and into the back of your neck, relaxing all the muscles of your neck, moving into your scalp, relaxing your scalp.

- This relaxing power is draining down slowly and gently into your face, down through your forehead, eyes, cheeks, mouth, jaw. Your jaw is relaxed. Your throat is relaxed. Your teeth slightly part. You are completely relaxed all over.

- Your entire body is now relaxed all over in every way. All tensions are gone from your body and mind. You are entirely relaxed and at ease.

- Continue deep slow breaths, until you feel your metabolism slowing down and feel your mind transcending into a deeper level of awareness.

- Allow your breathing to slow down now to a normal, even pace. Your breathing slows down. Allow your breathing to slowly reach a natural rhythm, until you begin to feel the deep silence within you.

I am relaxed and at ease.

PROTECTION

Awareness Enhancement Practice 2

White Light

For clarity and protection

Visualize a point of light far above you. See it in your mind's eye.

- See this light, a white light, flowing down and entering through the top of your head. Cosmic energy. A brilliant white light.

- As this light flows in through your mind and body, it fills you with perfect peace and perfect love. You feel totally serene and content.

- See this light fill your entire mind and body. See it glowing brilliantly as it radiates outward from the center of your body. Know that you are being revitalized with a vibrant energy.

- Now see this light expanding outward *beyond* your body, radiating outward, forming a bubble of white light all around you. Inside this bubble of white light, *know* that you are protected from all negativity. The white light cleanses you within and protects you without.

- See this bubble of white light clearly in your mind. Now see around it a band of golden light, a light of inspiration. And see around that a shield of brilliant blue light, an expanding shield. With this light—white light, golden light, and brilliant blue light—within you and around you, know that you are in perfect harmony with the universe.

- See this large bubble of light all around you, clearly in your mind's eye. Although you may not see it with your physical eyes, it is real. If you cannot visualize the light, *sense* it or *feel* its tingling energy.

Keep the white, gold, brilliant blue light around you at all times. This higher vibrational energy is a force-field shield for your protection.

You may also visualize this bubble of protective light around your life partner or mate, children, other family, friends, pets, home, possessions, car, office, school, anything and anyone.

Bubble of White Light Around Your Car

The white light is protection. It has saved me many times from physical harm, including potential automobile accidents. At least twice during icy winters in Colorado Springs, I lost control of my Mercury Comet and skid on ice. Immediately I let go of the steering wheel, removed my foot from the accelerator, threw my hands outward in a protective circle and *commanded* (without thinking) "STOP!"

It all happened at once: my *knowing,* the command, visualizing the light, asking for safety and protection, invoking the angels. The car spun and came to a stop—without injury and without crashing into any other vehicle or object.

The first time I learned to put white light around my car, I was new to this. It was after my awakening in 1975 but only months into studying with groups and learning metaphysical principles. On this first occasion, I had been dutifully placing a white light bubble around myself but had not yet learned to also place it around my car. On this first incident, I pulled out into a street after getting gas. Another car coming from my left ran into my driver-side door, crunching it in. I was uninjured. I slightly bumped my head on the window; it was nothing, not even a bruise, bump, or a headache. My car door and left front fender were crunched in, though. The damage stopped at *me.*

On many occasions since then, I have come within *inches* of being creamed. For me, it's always been the same: I automatically respond. I don't even think about it. All I know is, it works.

The White Light Rules

- Always keep the white light around yourself.

- Always place it around the vehicle you are traveling in.

- Place it around other people, pets, things, your home.

- *Know* the LIGHT is there.

- When danger strikes, *automatically* invoke THE LIGHT.

- Ask the angels for protection.

GROUNDING

Awareness Enhancement Practice 3

Centering

For balance and harmony

To maintain quality living and to be your full Self in the world: center. When centered, we are able to flow with the circumstances of life.

Difficult conditions and obstinate persons are opportunities to learn to flow in love. Each is an opportunity to learn harmony and to trust that we *are* taking the right steps along the way. When flowing with a full appreciation of a situation, we are not concerned with the outcome and we are able to allow others to be who they are.

Repeating affirmations out loud reinforces them in us (it doesn't have to be loud, just audible so you're not just thinking it).

You hear it. You feel it. It becomes a part of your body's experience ... so you remember it.

Say it to yourself as often as you wish and whenever you need it.

Whenever you encounter a difficult situation, take a moment to pause. Become still and calm. Then slowly affirm aloud to yourself:
I am still and aware.

Blessing to Begin the Day

The following Blessing to Begin the Day (may be used any time) can help heal you of despair and open you to love, to enjoying life and feeling truly happy. As you repeat it, visualize and *feel* the energy.

Once you can freely visualize this process, you may modify it to what works best for you—*felt* through your own resonance of the *knowing.* Actually *feel* the energy. Visualize:

- You are filled with the highest source of cosmic energy in the universe. Rejuvenated and renewed physically, mentally, spiritually, and emotionally.

- You are filled with the highest light, white light, divine light, glowing from within, effervescent.

> *I am a tree of light,*
> *rooted to the center of the earth,*
> *grounded through the soles of my feet,*
> *blossoming into the heavens through my crown,*
> *flowering.*
> *I am open and receptive,*
> *like a willow,*
> *flexible and bending for balance.*

- The light expands outward to surround you as an aura, a bubble of protective white light. Surrounded by golden light for illumination, wisdom, and understanding. Surrounded by a brilliant blue light for protection against all negativity.

- From your center, illuminating outward, a violet flame of the life force transmutes all energies about you into perfect love and magnifies this love ten thousand times ten thousand returned to you, manifesting harmony in all areas of your life: harmony in home, work, school, play; bringing prosperity, love, friendship, perfect companion, perfect health, peace of mind.

*All my needs are met
and all my wants are met
for the good of all,
according to the free will of all,
and I am one with all.
I am one.*

CLEARING

Awareness Enhancement Practice 4

Aura Cleansing

For inner peace and tranquility

The aura is a field of electromagnetic energy that emanates from the body and reveals the condition of physical, mental, emotional, and spiritual health. The aura reveals negative as well as positive thoughts, feelings, and behaviors. Cleansing our aura restores the polarity balance in our body and emotional self. Aura cleansing is a simple and effective way to rid ourselves of negative energies, whether ours or other people's we have picked up.

- Begin with slow, deep, rhythmic breaths. Relax. Be comfortable.

- Gently and gracefully stand. Lift your hands above your head. Face your palms toward each other. Gently brush your palms down the back of your head and shoulders, then gently over your ears and face. As you do this, say:

  I cleanse myself — mind, body, and spirit.

- Move your hands gently in slow graceful movements, like a dance. Let your sensitivity guide how much and where to cleanse your entire body, sweeping downward and around— front, sides, back—until you feel lighter, tingly, energized.

- Sweep the energy down and out your arms and hands now, past your fingertips. Shake off the "collected" energy like water. Visualize the energy dissipating, becoming nothing, becoming nonexistent.

You may wish to have a healer or a trusted friend cleanse your aura for you. Be sure both you and your friend mentally and physically shake off and *dissipate* all of the negative energy. See it going down into the earth, leaving you both filled with light.

Aura Cleansing with Crystals

Crystals are living organic forms that carry within them an imprint signature, and each crystal functions uniquely. They are especially potent for enhancing the human electro-magnetic field, cleansing, protecting, and aligning.

There are many different kinds of crystals. The amethyst is especially known for clearing negative energies and setting up a field of protection. A small one may be worn; a large amethyst crystal is more effective for an entire room. They also can be placed at doorways and windowsills. Choose a crystal (or gem stone) empathically (by feeling it), or by using psychometry or a pendulum, or a combination of these.

On two occasions, many years apart, channeling crystals have *come* to me. A channeling crystal has seven sides (known as windows) and is especially clear; it can magnify our connection to our Higher Self and enhance communication with higher consciousness. The first channeling crystal, I *found* when out for a walk at Bear Creek Canyon. After several years, it *felt* like time to give it away. A short time after I did, in 1983, I was walking in the woods in the Black Forest north of Colorado Springs when I happened to look down and at my feet was another channeling crystal. This one was three times larger than the one before and more clear. I asked at my host's house, but no one was missing it. I still have that crystal today and wear it every time I meditate and when I do intuitive readings.

When I have chosen crystals, on three occasions, I felt drawn to do so: twice at crystal shops, once from a friend who was giving away crystals. (There comes a time when you know your crystals have served their purpose and you pass them on.) When I choose crystals by *feeling* them (empathic sensation), I attune my intention (to find whatever crystals I need for whatever purpose unconsciously known to me at that time) and allow myself to be receptive.

Generally with my eyes closed, I slowly run my open palm over many crystals and allow myself to feel *pulled* to one in particular. You feel a subtle sensation; it's sort of magnetic. When you pick up the crystal (or gem stone), something triggers within you, a feeling of connection or sense of its purpose; you may feel a *buzz*. I often hear mentally (or intuit) a particular crystal's function and why it needs to be with me.

Crystals and gem stones are just another way to help yourself: increase your spiritual clarity, mental acuity, sensitivity, connection to your higher awareness. Human beings are electrical-magnetic. There is a connection between us and the elements of nature, through our electrical-magnetic fields. When we are attuned, there is some kind of connection between us. Rocks, crystals, and gem stones have their own unique magnetic properties.

If you don't feel anything at first, don't worry. Crystals are just another tool; and the empathic and intuitive senses are very subtle. When you're ready, you'll do it.

Another way to identify crystals that are meant for you is by using a pendulum over them. I also use a pendulum on occasion to determine my own subconscious or Higher Self answers when I can't be objective about making a decision. It's another tool. For me, the responses are generally very consistent and inform me more clearly just what I *really* want and what is *really* in my best interest.

When you first acquire a crystal, unless it's dug straight out of the earth it needs to be *cleansed* of prior human contact so you have a clean instrument that will imprint your personal vibration. (1) Bury the new crystal or gem stone in dry sea salt, or soak it in salt water, for at least twenty-four hours, then rinse it in cold water. Salt demagnetizes and rebalances the magnetic poles of the stone. (2) Then imprint it with your personal vibration. For a small crystal, wear it for about thirty days (until it feels *set*); you'll know when it's time to remove it because you'll start to feel jittery or excessively nervous—as if you have too much energy. At that point, only wear it to reconnect or re-energize and for sacred ceremonies, such as your daily meditation. To imprint a large crystal, keep it near (or under) your bed for a period of time. Or it may be appropriate to put it straight at the doorway or windowsill.

Another way to cleanse, renew, and charge crystals is running them under pure clear cold water, and visualize the crystal purifying. Also, because crystals are living organic substance, they resonate most clearly when often in contact with higher frequencies, such as fresh mountain streams, nature, and classical music. Nature is a powerful healing force and is symbiotic with humans.

ALIGNING

Awareness Enhancement Practice 5

Chakra Balancing

For alignment and to discover your purpose

Balancing the chakra centers results in higher consciousness, which is reflected in changed attitudes and values. There are seven major chakra *energy centers* associated with the physical body. Beginning at the bottom, their positions are: near the pubic bone, just below the belly button, just below the ribs, center of the chest, throat, center of the forehead, and top of the head (crown).

The *chakras* form a straight line up through the center of the body along the spine. Each energy center is several inches in diameter and is segmented much like the underflesh of a mushroom, and opens a portion at a time rather than as a whole.

It is unwise to hurry or force the opening of your chakras, such as by using drugs. To do so can result in psychic trauma or mental confusion because of the force of the cosmic energy bursting through. When any chakra opens, particularly the lower chakras, particularly the root or kundalini chakra, you need to be psychologically able to cope with any inrush of resurfacing unresolved emotional problems.

The *safe* way to open the chakras so the cosmic energy will flow smoothly through your body and consciousness is daily meditation, even if you don't feel anything happening while you're doing it. The chakras will open gradually at a pace that is right for you. Meditation is the natural and safe way to align body, mind, and spirit.

Although having a healer work with you is an effective way to clear your emotional blocks and to rebalance, meditation is a safe long-term method for clearing the energy centers yourself. Even with outside help, meditation is necessary for long-term effect, because no one else can do your inner work for you.

Another helpful tool is using a cassette program. It's sometimes easier to reach LEVEL with the help of an outside tool. I often use a cassette by Dick Sutphen, "Chakra Balancing and Energizing." It always regroups and grounds me.

Following is a chart of the chakra positions and endocrine glands—and associations I have intuited.[3]

Chakra Position	Association with Your Psyche	Endocrine Gland
7th Crown Top of head	Higher awareness Higher mind Accesses higher wisdom, channel Spirit	Pineal
6th Forehead "third eye"	Insight Clairvoyance, Psychic seeing	Pituitary
5th Throat	Interaction with world Communication	Thyroid
4th Heart	Compassion Empathic knowing, empathy Inner guidance, soul communication	Thymus
3rd Below ribs Solar Plexus	Creativity Mental premonition Sensing, "radar"	Pancreas
2nd Below belly button	Polarity Fears Relationships Relationships, childhood issues , family	Gonads
1st Root, base spine	Survival Sexuality, earthly desire	Adrenals

---

3   For more on chakras, read *Hands of Light*, Barbara Ann Brennan.

For balancing your chakras, which also clears and energizes them, I offer two original methods that *came* to me and I use for myself. The first is moving your hands before your body. The second is visualizing in your mind's eye while in a state of stillness. Before each exercise, *first* deep breathe, *then* cleanse your aura. Continue deep breathing gently throughout each technique, and visualize while following the directions. Move up from the bottom, clearing one chakra at a time.

Overlapping the palms polarizes the cosmic force and directs it to heal and balance. As you become familiar with how to do these chakra balancing movements, which is learned intuitively, you will have a mental picture of the energy's effect in your body.

Chakra Balancing Method 1

With your palms facing you, place your left hand over your right hand. Begin at the lowest chakra near the pubic bone.

- Hold your hands a few inches from your body. Allow your body-mind awareness to guide your arms and hands while you energize each chakra ... and for how long (seconds or minutes).

- Visualize a pulsing white light energy *beaming* from your palms *into* each chakra, charging that chakra with balancing energy.

- Move up to the second chakra energy center just below your belly button. Then to the chakra just below the center of your ribs. Then to the center of your chest. Then your throat. Then the center of your forehead. Then the top of your head.

- Once you have balanced all of these seven major chakras, move up *once more*—slowly—for a double charge. Visualize the pulsing energy beaming from your palms into your body. See the chakras pumping, like pistons.

- Now slightly part your palms, still facing toward the center of your body. Visualize energy beaming *from* your palms *into* and through your body. See energy rushing up and down through the center of your body through all of your chakras. Now beam that energy *into* your head and brain.

- When finished, gently press your palms and fingertips together and lay your hands comfortably in your lap. This will *contain* the energy for a while rather than allow it to dissipate too soon. Feel the vibrant energy circulating through you up and down. Maintain slow, even, deep rhythmic breaths.

- Now affirm:

  I am filled with light and wisdom.
  I receive the guidance I need at this time.

- See and feel the divine light flowing into and through you. Feel the vibrant energy of the universe flowing through you. You are now able to attune to your Higher Self or an Ascended Master.

Chakra Balancing Method 2

In a deeply relaxed state, having completed the deep breathing and prepared for meditation, see your root chakra as a ball of energy.

- Visualize that energy expanding and vibrating.

- Continue until you feel or sense the energy moving upward to the next chakra, which may take seconds or minutes.

Do each succeeding chakra. Belly button. Ribs. Chest. Throat. Forehead. Crown.

When clearing each chakra, you are raising a *path of light* straight up through the center of your being.

Continue this path of vibrant clear energy straight *above your head* to the *eighth* chakra for the Higher Self connection. With that chakra open, feel the path of energy pulling vertically as a *column of light* straight up. At this point, ask for guidance from your counselors. For example:

> *I open myself to the Spiritual Hierarchy and Masters of Wisdom.*
>
> *I ask for the help and counsel of my soul and angels, ascended guides, Teachers, and Masters.*

Continue with an affirmation, such as:

> *I am light. I am love. I am divinity.*
> *I am that I am.*
> *I am in the light.*
> *My work is in the light and only the light.*
> *I am love.*
> *I am.*
> *A–U–M ...*

You are now ready to meditate. Accept whatever *flows* to you as a gift from the Source.

Elaborate on, or change any steps or words in these exercises according to how your heart guides you. Continue affirming *"I am"* or *"I am love"* until you feel *at-one* and deep peace is flowing through you.

Another method for safely opening your chakra centers is repeating aloud to yourself the rd Psalm, which is a message to the weary and forgotten. Repeating this psalm opens chakra centers and attunes the inner sight and aura. It helps to perfect self-analysis, recover soul awareness and awareness of your full potential.

THE INNER STILLNESS

Awareness Enhancement Practice 6

Meditation

To feel the Divine Presence

The most useful activity for any day is meditation. Practiced diligently, more than any other spiritual activity, meditation enhances the process of integrating with our soul. Other activities are helpful, but none is as potent or effective as meditation.

Meditation is being *quiet within*, listening, allowing thoughts, images, and feelings to *float* in and through your mind during deep relaxation. By attuning to your center of peace and shutting out the world, you can receive insights and counsel from your Higher Self— that *still, small voice within.*

Observation is a key element. Meditation is tuning in to the life force. It is the easiest and safest way to find your center of peace, the center of your being, your core, your true Self.

Any kind of meditation is helpful. It is not what kind is right, but what works for *you.* With which style do you feel most comfortable? Which style takes you into your quiet inner place where you feel aligned and supremely connected to your divine Nature?

A **quiet meditation** is recommended for *beginners*: sitting still, without distractions.

An **active meditation** may be utilized at any level: with your body in movement.

Or you may meditate during **normal routines** of the day—very conscious every instant. This form is recommended only for *advanced* practitioners. Even when advanced, however, the *quiet time* is essential for continued development.

A *quiet meditation* is best practiced first thing in the morning—when you feel rested, your mind is clear, and the day's activities are before you. In this way, your mind is less jumbled and preoccupied. Also, having been recently asleep, you are still closely connected to the inner planes, so it is easier to access your Higher Self.

In the beginning, meditating approximately half an hour is recommended. Even once you have become disciplined, this is the approximate time frame that is the most productive. The reason for half an hour is because it takes a few minutes to settle in, a few minutes to get into focus and quiet the mind, a few minutes to connect, then time to *float* in the consciousness and the vibration ... just being there.

When meditating, *still* your expectations and quiet your admonitions to yourself. Do not anticipate any particular result. Do not assume that you must hear voices or see visions. This is not the usual experience. Meditation is a plane of inner being, within which you can sense the Divine Presence. Additional experiences are bonuses ... and they do come.

The purpose of meditation is to attune to your Higher Self, to become familiar with that energy and thereby able to invoke it throughout your daily life, at will. By the daily discipline of meditation, you can become familiar with your higher mind and that state of being. The *quiet time* teaches you how to recognize when you are in the energy and when you are not—for applying at all times in your daily life.

I sometimes play *The Eternal OM* (CD) during meditation when I need extra help to get into the deeper focus. I expect no particular result from any meditation, except the best I can give it on that day.

I also find that when I meditate daily, the meditations go deeper and stronger. If I miss a day, I usually need to regroup and rebuild the energy. Daily is most effective, and constancy gets the best results.

I find that my level or depth of connection fluctuates somewhat day by day, affected by my physical well-being and circumstances or concerns that may affect me mentally or emotionally. As a human being, I *am* sometimes pulled off center. I have found that for me the daily meditation is essential for being focused, clear, and aligned. I also have found that daily meditation gives me physical energy, smooths my personality concerns, alleviates my emotional distresses, and clears my mind. There are many benefits to meditation.

A focused and dedicated meditation—upon bringing the Higher Self viewpoint and influence into the personality—is incredibly powerful and continuously takes us to new heights. Focused dedication to oneness with the Divine strengthens the connection with the knowingness of *why we are here.*

Activities Essential to Wholeness

Daily disciplines in attitudes

- Learning to forgive yourself of errors. Not to judge your actions as good or bad. Not to judge other people's actions as right or wrong.

- *Emotionally* accessing equilibrium and equanimity. Learning not to rise into ecstasy, nor fall into despair. Learning to maintain a sense of harmony and balance in everything you do, no matter what kind of experience it is.

- *Mentally* being open to expanding your perceptions of reality. Being open to exploring new attitudes and a new consensus of opinion; if nothing else, as a comparative study.

- *Physically* is important because the more aligned we are physically, the easier it is to function at our best. For physical alignment, clear your mind and energize your body with fresh air and exercise. Abstain from substances that abuse the body or create dysfunction, such as food allergies. This also means moderation in medications that may cause an imbalance in the body. Monitor how your *whole being* feels.

Stilling the Mental Chatter in Your Mind

These four methods are helpful during meditation to tune out sounds, interference, and disturbances.

1. ***Sit straight.*** Sit in a yogi position, or with your feet flat on the floor, or on a meditation bench. Keep your spine straight to allow your energy to flow smoothly and clearly; your mind is more clear, and it is easier to let go of mental distractions.

2. ***Connect your thumb and forefinger on each hand*** (or thumb and middle finger, or all three). This connection changes the flow of your energy.

   Or: Lay your hands in your lap, palms faced upward; or thumbs and forefingers touching, each hand separately; or palms together in front of you, prayer position, either close or far, before your heart, throat, forehead or above your crown. All of these can take place during a single sitting. *Let your hands move where they will.*

   Or: Palms clasped, fingers interlocked, close to you, before your heart. Why connect your palms in the prayer position or clasping? To me, this feels like bonding the magnetic poles of the body (polarity). After a time, the connection between the palms becomes energized and magnetized. This is one way I determine how deep I am in the consciousness. Also, it feels good. The energy enhances, and I feel a much stronger connection to the Divine Presence.

   Allow your hands to hold whatever position they will throughout a meditation, because the body and inner Self know what is needed to make the connection on any given day. Do not restrict yourself to any particular mode of sitting or stance. Allow your body to follow its own rhythm.

3. **Deep breathe.** Breathe slowly and evenly in deep *rhythmic* breaths. Breathe deeply in and out through *both* nostrils simultaneously—along the *back* of your throat.

   With your mouth closed, very slowly and gradually inhale and exhale—as deeply as you can—until you discover your rhythm. A continued rhythmic pattern of deep breaths will move you beyond the chatter, not discarding or ignoring it, but moving past it, *through* it.

   Since I began channeling my Higher Self (oversoul) in 1982, all written materials have emphasized the importance of *breath* for cleansing, healing, and integrating with the Higher Self. *Deep and full belly breathing is the easiest tool for reaching the deeper consciousness.*

   If you do not yet know a breath technique, many people teach the healing breath. For example, I first encountered using *breath* during a six-week course of hatha yoga in July 1975, only months before my spontaneous awakening to cosmic consciousness in October when I found myself automatically and unconsciously using a breath rhythm, although it evolved into my own method.

4. **Simultaneously focus attention on your third eye.** Feel the energy in the center of your forehead (just above your brow), even when you are going through all your body's energy centers (chakras).

MEDITATION STYLES

These processes *came* to me and work for me. You may already be familiar with any or all of these techniques. I offer them for those of you who are not.

Attunement is sensed. By a trembling vibration, the energy of the universal force, you know when you have reached the *union.*

Allow the wisdom that comes into your mind. This is *your* inner guidance, your inner voice.

Basic Meditation

After a few minutes of the following meditation, think about the impressions you had. What did you see in your inner vision? What thoughts or words did you hear spoken into your mind? What insights or awarenesses did you perceive or sense? Write these down now (or record them onto a cassette during the meditation).

It is recommended to keep a journal and date each entry. Keep it in a handy place where you can jot down any insights that occur to you throughout the day.

Meditation does more than quiet the mind. It enhances inner communication with our divine Nature.

- Sit in a quiet place, undisturbed, with your feet flat on the floor and your back straight. Take several long, deep breaths to release stress and tension. Allow your body to relax and become comfortable.

- Sink deeply into meditation now. Allow thoughts and images to float into and *through* your mind. Allow impressions to float. Do not try to control or change your thoughts. Just observe, listen, and allow. Let go.

- Allow yourself to lull into deep relaxation, drifting gently. You will commune with your Higher Self or a Spiritual Teacher.

- Get comfortable. Settle in. Feel your body relaxing ... all the way from your toes up through the top of your head.

- Take several even, long, deep breaths. Then breathe out slowly. Feel yourself drifting into deeper relaxation with each slowing breath. Feel the breath cleansing and healing you. Feel your spirit becoming free. Feel your mind becoming free. Let the breath guide you into deep deep serenity, deep peace and tranquility. Relax ... sink ... sigh ... let go.

- Breathe slowly, deeply, long. Warm ... secure ... aware. Letting go ... flowing.

- Release your body. Release your mind. You are one with the universe.

I am one with the universe.

- Breathe deeply into the stillness, deeply into the silence, deeply into the center of your being.

I am one with the universe.

- Tingling ... humming ... resonating ... radiating ... filling with light.

- Your heart is radiating ... warm and full. You are love. You are still, calm, and serene. Be still and listen. Listen to the silence.

I am one with the universe.

- Take a moment now and mentally ask a question that concerns you. Listen for the answer that comes *into* your mind.

- All right. Release ... allow ... flow ... let go.

- Release with breath ...

Deeper Relaxation Meditation

Deeper relaxation is most beneficial for stilling an overactive mind or hassled body, for when you are feeling wound up or uptight.

Remember, whenever you induce deeper relaxation, you are in full control at all times. You can return to full waking consciousness simply by moving the index finger of your left hand. Or you can slip into a natural deep sleep.

- You have already cleansed your aura.

- You are breathing slowly, evenly, and deeply.

- Now feel your body's metabolism slowing down and begin to fully relax.

- Your body is beginning to relax. Feel the relaxing power coming into your toes, relaxing your toes.

- Feel the relaxing power moving up through your feet, calves, thighs, legs ... relaxing. Warm relaxing power. Warm relaxing power.

- Now feel this relaxing power coming into the fingers of your hands, relaxing your hands. Relaxing your forearms. Relaxing your upper arms. Relaxing.

- Feel this relaxing power beginning to flow upward through your spine ... through all the organs of your body, relaxing your entire body. Relaxing your stomach muscles. Relaxing all the muscles of your back.

- Feel this relaxing power moving up through your shoulders and into the back of your neck, relaxing all the muscles of your neck. Moving up into your scalp, relaxing your scalp.

- Now feel this relaxing power draining down gently into your face. Down through your forehead, eyes, cheeks, jaw, mouth. Relaxing your jaw. Your throat is relaxed. Your teeth slightly part. You are completely relaxed, completely relaxed.

- Your entire body is now relaxed all over, in every way. All tensions are gone from your body and mind. You are entirely relaxed and at ease.

Meditation in Motion

The body loves the rhythm of slow musical movements. For busy, active people who like to be on the go and have trouble slowing down, spontaneous dancing and chanting is a style of meditation that *came* to me at the onset of my awakening. Although I was naturally letting my body follow its own rhythm, I later discovered that the movements were like Tai Chi—although I had never taken a class (so it was either soul memory or an innate rhythm of the aligned spirit in the body).

Tai Chi is an ancient Chinese martial art used as dance for integrating the body, mind, and spirit.

Meditation-in-motion may also be similar to Sufi dancing, or any other long forgotten (non-Western) ritualistic spiritual or folk dance. Meditation-in-motion helps to relax the body and clear the mind. Absorbed by the music, you feel only the music's vibration and you are able to more easily shut out noises and distractions. The spontaneous movements come as you *free flow.* The movements are natural and seem to come automatically.

Specific practices may come to you while dancing, such as cleansing your aura, third eye, or spine. Even if these movements seem silly or unfamiliar, they are important. You may do arm or body movements for months before realizing their benefit or the reason. They just feel good. Each movement you find yourself doing serves a purpose for your spirit and body: moving the energies of your vibration and environment to cleanse and heal you.

You may know the meaning of your movements immediately or only after continued practice. Certain images or memories may float into your awareness while your body moves. You may have an intuitive understanding of how each movement is affecting your body and spirit. Yet while some basic cleansing movements are helpful, you need not plan them. Allow your body-mind to direct you. You will naturally do what your body and aura need.

The movie *Isadora,* starring Vanessa Redgrave as Isadora Duncan, is about a free-form dancer in the early 1900s in Europe and Britain. Redgrave's youthful performance captures the innocence and free-spirit essence of Isadora, who frequently wore, both on stage and off, delicate draping Aphrodite frocks and crowns of garlands. Redgrave's dancing, which is abundant throughout the film and for which Isadora was famous, is reminiscent of meditation-in-motion as I have experienced it. Isadora says in the film that she has beauty inside her and she knows she is to give this beauty to others through dance. Her dancing is natural and spontaneous and comes from the heart. It flows from her as a oneness with the spirit of life.

If you lead a busy, hectic life and find it difficult to sit still for meditation, or if you would like to try this alternate method, put on some soothing music (such as Japanese, flute, harp, Jean-Pierre Rampal, Paul Horn, Ravi Shankar) and push back your furniture to create more space for free-flowing movements. Once you have read the following directions, close your eyes (preferably) to block out distractions, then let the rhythm take over.

- Sway to the music's rhythm until you feel at-one with the music.

- Slow, even movements, in and out, back and forth. Slow and steady, your whole body, any movement your body wants to make.

- Hang loose. Feel the music caressing you. Feel its gentle vibration. Flow with it. *Move until your body moves for you.*

- Feel the energy tingling in your hands, then moving through your arms and entire body, gentling pushing and pulling.

- Move in a circle, your entire body moving up and down, your back loose, arms and head loose, knees loose, legs loose, up and down.

- When you are ready, quiet your movements. Slowly sit on the floor and cross your legs to begin spontaneous chanting. (You may also chant while dancing.)

- Speak or sing whatever sounds or words flow from you. The words may not be in your native language. They may sound like nonsense. They may be the language of an ancient time or the language of the soul. Allow your *supra*-conscious mind to speak.

- Chant what flows. Feel the peace of the songs you chant. Allow the chanting to slowly fade into silence.

A modified form of spontaneous dance is sitting with legs crossed and moving your hands, arms, and upper torso. Spontaneous dancing and chanting in a group unifies everyone, leaving them feeling they have shared something special. Being spontaneous teaches higher sensitivity. Meditation-in-motion teaches you to let go and flow.

Following is an example of my own spontaneous chanting (English translation intuited, each line repeated several times):

Ki-ee-i yo see ko, Lo-ee-ah tee oh, O yo-see-ko
Holy one, my Father, Great Father, Our Father

You may wish to chant A–U–M ... *or* AA–RE–OHM ... *or* OHM ... *or* AH.

To Go Deeper

Clasp your hands before you, or in the prayer position. Breath *slowly* and steadily—in along the *back* of your throat.

- As you breathe, while focusing on a seed thought like a mantra, sound the A–U–M (or OHM). Feel the energy moving through and around you, and visualize the energy patterns.

- Focus only on the seed thought. Let all else float away. *Always come back to the seed thought.*

- Feel yourself going deeper and deeper. Feel your consciousness slowing down.

- Focus your mind on the seed thought for as long as it feels right—until you feel the energy *shift* (30-40 days).

- Let go of any expectations of what the seed thought means. Just *experience* it. Just release yourself to it, knowing that your inner mind will guide you.

The Best Part

Step by step, seed thought by seed thought, not only will you change within, but your experiences in the outer world will also change. This meditation will affect not only your spiritual life (the vertical) but also your human life (the horizontal). It is very powerful and transforming.

When I meditate every day, I am most consistently attuned throughout the day (more focused, calm, trusting, happy). A wonderful benefit is that at any time during the day, when I am focused on work or real-life matters, the inner voice sends me a short mes*sage (usually a phrase) to answer any number of pressing concerns. I write them down, so I won't forget the *insight.* I have learned to trust these insights—so that once I know *what* will happen regarding any life matter I wonder about, or the best course of action for me: decision made. I accept and move on. I no longer need to dwell on the issue, as I know what I must do. This frees me from excessive worry or over-thinking. It releases the burden of uncertainty.

A clear *insight* that spontaneously pops into my mind when I am busy with other matters—living life—is the inner guidance that keeps everything running smoothly. I feel in harmony, as I have learned that I can let go and trust the choice or course of action recommended. The insights are usually brief, succinct; may be one word ("yes," "no") or a short phrase ("a contract in April," "a black man in the White House" [received in October 2008, before the election of Barack Obama]).

These three meditation styles, as well as the advanced meditation styles in Part III, are suggested methods. There are many available in the world, including Transcendental Meditation which I often channel-advise to people during intuitive readings. The wise approach as a beginner is to follow suggested practices. As you become familiar with what is available, it is beneficial to try different forms for getting to the deep inner quiet place within your own being.

Actually there are many ways to meditate: including through nature, hiking, walking, jogging, Tai Chi, Zen—basically whatever works for you. The only real rule is to listen to your own body, your *yen.* What do you *want* to do? That is *your* way.

MEDITATION SCRIPT

Attuning to the Inner Stillness

When this exercise ends, you may awaken or continue meditating, or go into a natural deep sleep.

As you deep breathe, affirm:

I am still and aware.

- Inhale several long, deep even breaths, inhaling through your nose from the depths of your diaphragm (belly). Air rises slowly into your lungs. Inhale until you can inhale no more. Hold for a few seconds. Then exhale slowly, allowing every breath to leave your body, until there is no breath left.

- Continue deep breathing. Each breath takes you deeper and deeper into soul consciousness. You drift into full awareness. A wave of warm relaxation flows throughout your body. You are totally relaxed and at ease.

- As your body slows down, your mind transcends to a deeper level of awareness. Your breathing slows to a normal even pace and you are in the *soul state of consciousness.*

See a light far above you.

- The white light now flows down and enters the top of your head. This cosmic energy flows through your body and mind. You are filled with perfect peace and love. You are totally serene and content. The light fills your body and mind, glowing as it flows.

  I am revitalized with vibrant energy, in body, mind, and spirit.

- The light expands outward from you as an aura, forming a bubble of protective white light around you. You are cleansed within and protected from without from all negativity.

- See this bubble of pure white light clearly in your mind. Around it is a band of golden light. Around both is a shield of brilliant blue light. With this white light, golden light, and blue light, within you and around you, you are in perfect harmony with the cosmic energies of the universe.

  I am filled with the highest source of cosmic energy in the universe. Rejuvenated and renewed physically, mentally, spiritually, and emotionally.

  I am filled with the highest light, white light, divine light, glowing from within, effervescent.

  I am a tree of light, rooted to the center of the earth, grounded. As a willow, flexible and bending for balance.

  All of my needs are met and all of my wants are met, for the good of all, according to the free will of all, and so it is.
  I am one with all. I am one.

Now balance your chakras.

- Imagine a path of light moving up from the center of the earth through your feet and legs to your root chakra. See a ball of energy expanding and vibrating.

- In a few seconds or minutes, the energy moves up a path of light to your second chakra below the belly button. See the energy expanding and radiating.

- The energy moves up the path of light to your third chakra below your ribs. See the energy expanding and radiating.

- The energy continues up the path of light to your fourth chakra at your heart, your chest. Imagine and feel the energy expanding and radiating outward from your center, opening your heart and clearing away all sadness ... opening you to peace.

- The energy continues up the path of light to your throat chakra. See and feel the energy expanding and radiating.

- The energy continues up the path of light to your third eye chakra at your forehead. See and feel the energy expanding and radiating. You are feeling more and more calm.

- The energy continues up the path of light to your crown chakra. See and feel the energy expanding and radiating. You feel clear and in harmony.

- The energy continues up the path of clear white radiating light through the center of your being. The light continues up through the Higher Self chakra just above your head.

- As you see and sense the energy expanding and radiating, feel it *connect.* A resonance begins to *hum* within you. Feel a center of strength straight up through you. Your mind is clear. You are in perfect peace.

• Open yourself to Spirit. Ask for the help and counsel of all your spirit guides, Ascended Teachers and Masters. Ask for the help of your angels and oversoul. Ask for the help of the Masters of Wisdom.

> *I am light. I am love. I am divinity.*
> *I am that I am.*
> *I am in the light.*
> *My work is in the light and only the light.*
> *I am love.*
> *I am.*
> *A–U–M.*
>
> *I am still.*
> *Divine light flows through me.*
> *The vibrant energy of the universe flows into me.*
> *I now attune to my Higher Self and Spiritual Master.*
> *I am filled with light and wisdom.*
> *I receive the guidance I need at this time.*

Now sink deeply into meditation.

• Allow thoughts, images, and impressions to float into and through your mind—and let them go. Simply observe and listen. Lull into deep relaxation now, gently drifting into meditation, wherein you may commune with your Higher Self or Spiritual Teacher or Master.

• You are comfortable and settled. Your body is relaxed. Your mind is calm. You are *still*.

> *I am still.*

- Take several long deep breaths and let them out slowly. Drift deeper into relaxation with each breath.

- The breath is cleansing and healing, the breath guides you into deep deep serenity, deep deep peace and tranquility.

The deep breaths are soothing,
releasing my body,
releasing my mind.
I am one with all life.

I breathe deeply into the stillness,
deeply into the silence,
deeply into the center of my being.

My being is tingling,
humming,
resonating.

Warmth is filling me.
My heart is radiating love.

I listen.
I listen to the silence.

I am serene.
Calm.
Still.

Part III

Heightened Intuition

The teachings in this section are from various manuscripts received through the Universal Consciousness 1982-1994 (including *The New Humans: Second Genesis,* and a subsequent books (in production).

NEW UNIVERSAL LAWS

For Our Modern Times

"Tenets of Clear Being"

The "Tenets of Clear Being" *came* to me from the Universal Consciousness in 1994 for *The Soul Path*. These basic tenets are guidelines to help us awaken our inner light and integrate our divine essence in daily life. The "Tenets" are formulas to raise our spiritual vision and whole potential.

The first version, "Principles of Balanced Being," came in 1982, immediately following the spontaneous completion of my oversoul-merge process (integrating with my personality, which took six-and-a-half years, November 2, 1975 to March 5, 1982).[4]

Both versions of these new Universal Laws came independently, separately, and spontaneously. Yet, the "Tenets" are parallel to and paraphrase the order *and* theme of the "Principles." Although twelve years apart, both versions are identical in concept and written in the same order, only in different words.

See the comparison charts below.

---

4   The "Principles of Balanced Being" were first published in a limited spiral-bound edition for workshop participants and a few close friends from *Visions of Serendipity*, the early draft of soon-to-be-published *Angels of Serendipity*.

1994 - Tenets of Clear Being
1. Be in the moment that you are.
2. Be exactly where you are.
3. Acknowledge your highest level of being.
4. Appreciate yourself.
5. Appreciate others.
6. Exude a clear presence.
7. Invoke a clear conscience.
8. Honor the highest range of affection.
9. Live in the beliefs of goodwill.
10. Give of yourself when needed.

1982 - Principles of Balanced Being
1. Live in the time of NOW.
2. Live in the space I AM.
3. At all times, dwell in the spirit and not in the flesh.
4. Know that you are what you believe yourself to be.
5. Balance giving and receiving.
6. Vibrate a clear tone.
7. Harmonize with all.
8. Be love.
9. Release all that does not heal.
10. Serve others when inspired to serve.

Essence of the 10 New Universal Laws
1. Being present
2. Self-acceptance
3. Living in consciousness
4. Self-image
5. Giving and receiving
6. Sound (vibration)
7. Oneness with all
8. Self-love
9. Sacrifice
10. Service

1. *Be in the moment that you are.*

This is the law of *being present,* to coordinate our activities to flow one from the other, so that we feel at-one with all.

2. *Be exactly where you are.*

This is the law of *self-acceptance,* to change our situation by changing our attitude. Space and reality are what we perceive them to be. The blocks we feel around us, we create by our own desires. We have only to *desire* a situation different for it to transform.

3. *Acknowledge your highest level of being.*

This is the law of *living in consciousness,* wherein we are our true essential Self. We are not only flesh. We are body, mind, and spirit. Spirit is our vital force, our breath, our essence. In our spirit, we see clearly, as the angels see; we express our higher Nature, live our higher calling, understand and perceive all that which is designated by the angels.

4. *Appreciate yourself.*

This is the law *of self-image.* When we believe we are good and true, that becomes our nature. When we believe we are dark or evil, that becomes our nature. When we think we are spiritually blind, it is because we believe that. Our belief is the greater power.

5. *Appreciate others.*

This is the law of *giving without expectation* and *receiving with gratitude;* both giving and receiving to be in balance. We are all equal in the Great Forever. No one is greater than any other.

6. *Exude a clear presence.*

This is the law of *sound,* or *energy.* Sound is vibration. Vibration is in all living things, in all time. Vibration is the essence that links all living things. Our essence is vibration-tone-resonance-sound-light-breath-spirit. We can *know* our Higher Self through our breath. Our essential Nature vibrates in us when we are aligned and our tone is clear.

Our aura is an energy field of light. The angels help us clarify our aura so we can understand *how* to flow beyond our dense illusions. The angels do not speak with external sound; however, when we are clear, we are able to hear their thoughts to us and perceive their presence as easily as we perceive our own breath.

7. *Invoke a clear conscience.*

This is the law of *oneness with all brethren,* to harmonize with others through synchronistic breathing during inner communion. In breath, all are one. We grow through the efforts of the people and spirits around us. Therefore, it is wise to seek harmony with them. It is wise not to see ourselves or any other as incomplete; rather, to open to our vision and remember that all of our supposed errors are blindness to our true Self and true potential.

8. *Honor the highest range of affection.*

This is the law of *self-love.* We find I AM Consciousness through *being* love. In love, we release. In love, we allow. In love, we let go. In love, we set no barrier and we set no end. When we remember that all are equal, we *are* love. The more we accept our innate goodness, the more we accept ourselves in love, live our goodness, and see others through the eyes of love. We learn to be love. We learn through the *breath* how love feels, what it feels like to receive love, and what it feels like to give love.

9. *Live in the beliefs of goodwill.*

This is the law of *sacrifice*—sacrificing only that which is not the whole. This is honoring our essential Self and the essential nature of all living things. When we are bound out of our inner essential Nature, it feels like a sacrifice to give up our appetites. Yet there is no true giving up of what is not for our whole good. To choose wisely and not be ruled by our appetites, we submit to the truth of our Higher Self. We connect with our Higher Self through synchronistic *breathing* in inner communion. We meditate without expectation and without thought ... as though there is only this one hour. When you commune, affirm: *"I Am."*

10. *Give of yourself when needed.*

This is the law of *service*. As an equal aspect of The Breath, we give of ourselves in service, not for gain but because we value the light of every soul and we give from our heart without thought of reward. Our essential Nature brings people to us who need what we have to give. Serve all equally. It matters not *how* we serve, only that we serve—in light—and serve all who come to us.

Each person chooses whether he or she will live by these Universal Laws. Therefore, we are advised not to determine that any other do so, because only a self who chooses freely commits to *being* love and freely *lives* the Universal Laws ... because they are felt in the heart.

The Divine Mind says to us: "Keep these commandments with justice and with love. Be not a tyrant. Do not ordain yourself as a lawmaker or a lawbreaker. Do not set yourself above any other. Live these Laws only for yourself, because obedience and understanding cannot be forced."

When we live by the Laws of the universe, we are expressing our essential Self.

GUIDELINES FOR USING THE SPIRITUAL POWER

Spiritual power is the result of oneness with our true Self. Being spiritual means living a life of integrity and honor, measured by our sense of value and worth.

We *re-acquire* the divine state by acknowledging our innate Nature. We free ourselves of the poverty of consciousness by breathing effortless devotion into our *creative* nature. When we apply the knowledge and wisdom inherent in creative release, works of art carry a healing vibration that reaches out and touches others with the magnificence. That is spiritual power.

The Divine Mind says that this power is binding on two counts: One, it is acquired only by one who has begun to perceive *unity.* Two, it can be used only for beneficent results for the good of the many. No harm can come from such a gift or else the gift is canceled by will of the Greater Lights. The power, while personal, is attained by one who has agreed to live by Universal Law yet is able to reach beyond the laws of Earth to manifest a greater freedom. Only those who have attained vision can manifest such a power.

The following lists, written from the Infinite Consciousness of the Divine Mind, identify positiveness in outlook. These lists are only a beginning and are not meant to be an end of anyone's consideration. As we become more attuned to our true self and to the community, the Divine Mind suggests that we personally add to these lists and continue adding to them as we evolve and mature in the use of spiritual energy. These lists are merely a means of categorizing ideas. They are not meant to limit our focus. They are given to stimulate potentialities of personal expression. By following the ideas in these lists, we can become filled with the light of the supreme spiritual power, says the Divine Mind.

When we attain spiritual access to the Universal Laws of life, we are given guidance regarding the use of the Force for transforming reality. Freedom of thought is given to anyone who has learned to accept self. Freedom of action is a reward for dedicated service to Spirit.

Now, some of the ways in which the *spiritual power* can be used to enhance your personal reality and community.[5]

---

5   These spiritual insights are from my book *Global Society 2.0*, received through my oversoul consciousness in 1985 and first published here (now in production, in *"The New Humanity"* Series).

Spiritual Power Guideline 1

To Be Spiritually Aware

- Allow soul to fill you.

- Be grateful for each day that you live.

- Accept that you are choosing.

- Look to yourself for answers, to others for ideas upon which to build your own decisions.

- Choose friends by the contentment you feel with them.

- Accept change.

Spiritual Power Guideline 2
To Embody the Divine Inner Light

- Embrace the light.

- Believe in your inner being.

- Actualize the power.

- Integrate the divine *at-one-ment.*

- Be aware that you have clear seeing, allow it to work for you, follow your insight and sensibility in each encounter.

- Trust and allow your inner voice, that you already have the ability to clearly receive telepathically (clairaudiently).

- Practice the Tenets of Clear Being (the Principles of Life, Universal Laws).

- Energize your body and mind through thoughtfulness, appreciation, and thanksgiving.

- Allow your problems. Appreciate them, then let them go. Remember always that the answers are within.

Spiritual Power Guideline 3

To Access the Inner Power

Spiritual power and inner strength are accessed through union with the I AM. The voice of the I AM is a quiet voice heard in the *stillness* of our breath.

- Let the angels help you.

- Release negative feelings to the Divine Essence within. Visualize white light entering the top of your head and radiating outward from your being, healing and transmuting all negativity.

- Forgive.

- Be discrete in what you speak and to whom.

- Trust your highest potential.

- Be kind.

- Daily cleanse your mind, aura, and body.

- Meditate.

- Pray for guidance, protection, and wise counsel.

- Affirm your strength.

- Affirm your power.

- Love yourself:

I transcend my past.
I know where I have been and where I'm going.
I am open to being whole.
I am affectionate.
The I AM moves through me.
I am free.
I am whole.
I am divine.
I love myself.
I am.

Spiritual Power Guideline 4

To Accumulate the Spiritual Power

Some elements for developing spiritual assessment

- Deeply appreciate the forces of nature.

- Live in harmony with all peoples.

- Develop sensory awareness of your physical and emotional bodies.

- Acquire knowing of the environment you are in.

- Pursue your natural freedom of choice in selecting a path of work.

- Balance joyful activities with daily responsibilities.

- Align free will with the good of all around you.

- Develop, through ritual practice, an aura of reformed focus.

- Send good thoughts.

- Depend on your inner voice.

- Listen to the good council of others.

Spiritual Power Guideline 5

To Transmute the Spiritual Power

Transmuting spiritual truth, transmuting power to spiritual freedom

- Create a synergy of mind and body.

- Prepare your body to function daily without excesses or indulgence.

- Train your feelings for restored laughter.

- Join belief with will.

- Complete personal ambition.

- Release anger.

- Atone for all misjudgments.

- Reach out and become a participant in life.

- Enlist thought as a means of sound beliefs.

- Cancel false desires.

- Resolve karma.

Spiritual Power Guideline 6

To Use the Spiritual Power Practically

- Devise an overview of your needs.

- Qualify desire from ambition.

- Apply others' insights.

- Restrain emotional excitement that nurtures confusion.

- Acquire a complete breathing rhythm.

- Adjust your environment to suit your plan.

- Set up a complete list of sources.

- Believe.

- Follow your inner voice.

- Receive natural magic.

- Arrange willed results in order of importance to the whole.

- Confirm ambition as a clearly perceived focus with intent to heal.

- Bring others into consultation for a broad perception.

- Form a clear outline for results.

- Entice yourself to understanding natural magic.

- Practice every day the integration of the forces of life with your mind, spirit, and body.

Spiritual Power Guideline 7

To Use the Spiritual Power to Enhance your Personal Reality

- Focus on pleasing yourself.

- Realign yourself to conscious decision-making through intuitive knowing.

- Tell others what you will into your reality.

- Allow others to help you if they wish.

- Seek not conformity but individuality.

- List personal needs and wants, to draw a clear plan of intent.

- Itemize your desires and wishes.

- Simplify your personal needs by determining the greater good.

- Listen to the inner voice.

- Find out who you are.

- Accomplish your dreams with the support of friendship.

- Acquire peaceful negotiation as a means of attainment.

Spiritual Power Guideline 8

To Use the Spiritual Power for the Community Reality

- Realize you are one of many who has the same focus of intent in this reality.

- Achieve oneness with the group focus.

- Learn to negotiate and settle according to the greater good of all.

- Send forth concepts for practical analysis.

- Consider the group as an energy focus for general reward and benefit.

- Listen to the needs of others.

- Make certain that your needs are not in conflict with the needs of the whole.

- Simply be available for support and assistance to the group energy.

- Acquire a good standing and rapport with those around you.

- Jump not to conclusions, but analyze and consider, before you process choices.

- Keep problems to yourself. Do not spread bad news or bad feelings. Dissipate these through the Divine Energy within.

- Choose sensory modifiers that demonstrate your willingness to join the cooperative effort.

- Believe in the good of the whole.

- Align yourself with others in personal exchanges.

EXTRA-STRENGTH PROTECTION

Against All Forces

We are subject to outer influences only when we allow them.

Physical rituals help set a protecting energy in a space. Examples are smudging with natural sage, ringing a sacred bell throughout the space, thrusting your power outward in all directions throughout the space (as I did to move the flash flood), burning white candles, prayer, asking angels and/or God for guidance and protection.

Mental rituals include visualization, meditation, and intuition-development tools such as in this book. (Additional powerful resources are a cassette "Banishing Evil" by Jonathan Parker, Gateways Institute; and the book *Psychic Self Defense and Well-Being* by Melita Denning and Osborne Phillips.)

Very important rituals: daily aura clearing, visualizing the bubble of white light around you, daily meditation, crystals.

Especially important: Visualize a bubble of white light around you in the morning, anytime you feel stressed, afraid or worried; and before you go to sleep at bedtime. Visualize the protective white light and the presence of guardian angels around you, your loved ones, and your home. Invite the angels to be with you. The angels are with you.

The angels are with me.

How to Identify a Presence

By setting the protection before you sleep, you strengthen your ability to avert any outside forces when you are not consciously in your body.

For example, one time I visited a man who was in state prison in Canyon City, Colorado. He had telephoned me to help him get rid of dark spirits that were haunting him. I took a man friend with me, who was more experienced in such matters. After the one meeting at the prison, a couple of times I had a "dream" that the convict was trying to enter my house—but he couldn't get past the door because of a protective light shield around my home. On waking each time, I *knew* this had been a real psychic visitation. (The few times I have actually seen myself in a dream in the real place where I was sleeping, I knew intuitively these were true psychic visitations and not subconscious dreams.) The convict never tried to "visit" me again. That was the end of it.

Some people feel a presence, which may be a spirit, ghost, or entity. *Spirits* are nonphysical beings who live beyond the physical realm. *Ghosts* are stuck between realms and have not moved on to the higher realities after death of the physical body; often, they can be assisted to realize they have died and instructed to move toward the light where loved ones await them. *Entities* may be unfriendly or even malicious and may have misdirected intentions and desires (not unlike some people in the world).

It is important to know how to feel a presence. If it is a positive presence, you will benefit from being able to recognize that the spirit is with you to help you in some way (this is the most common experience, as with angel vibrations which give a tingling sensation throughout the body). In the case of a presence that is negative or potentially harmful, it is wise to be aware of subtle nonphysical *sensations,* then to discern their *origin.*

You can tell mainly by how you *feel,* whether a being (or person, place, opportunity) is positive. If your energy feels expansive, glowing, joyful—it's pretty good guess that spirit is beneficial. If you feel darkness, ugliness, inclined to shrink, pull away from, withdraw, that energy is best to avoid, send away or CANCEL. If you just feel nervous from lack of experience but nothing overt is happening, let it go. *Focus on:* meditation and being in your light. That alone is *very* powerful.

When you meditate to seek more awareness about a presence you sense around you, remember that impressions are generally subtle.

Identify the energy field. You may feel different sensations related to different kinds of energy forces in the environment, both tangible and intangible. Focus on the specific energy presence you feel. Think about how it feels. What impressions occur to you or flash through your mind? Do you feel a physical sensation? (That is your personal signal of that specific presence.)

For example, I get tingling or chills all over my body as confirmation (from angels) of a truth (it can also be a certain part of the body). This is very different from suddenly feeling like I want to throw up. Different energies. One you want. The other you want to walk away from or get rid of. (This also pertains to people and places.)

At the same time as feeling an energy, request the identity of the *voice* speaking. Ask, *"Who are you?"* Any entity or being *must* answer. If you are not sure of the kind of being it is, ask *"Are you of the light?"* Asking "Are you of the Christ, God, the Divine?" or some such divine name will also draw an important answer to help you identify if the being is anything other than beneficial. All beings *must* answer.

Turn your focus to clear light. Sense whether the being lives by the laws of light. Allow attunement only with light and love. Depend on your inner guidance; at the same time, evaluate and discern the source. Most beings we feel are beneficial, but it is always wise to be discerning, just as it is with people. Be sensible, and use intuitive common sense.

Another way to get information on a presence visiting you is to focus during a state of hypnosis or self-hypnosis (by using a recorded guided exercise) in which you can go into another level of awareness where your perceptions are more keenly attuned to nonphysical realities. It is a good idea to record whatever impressions come to you during the session, to validate your experience. You may be surprised at the details (you will probably forget them if you don't record them). Most likely, you will receive some sort of tangible confirmation within days if not hours. Confirmation often shows up in odd ways, as if out of the blue: a person says something that rings true, or something happens that triggers your awareness beyond words.

One thing is sure, with the psychic realm it is seldom possible or easy to verify details the way we want them. Most often, it's something we just know is true. With practice and experience, you learn to trust what you know. When things bear out over and over, you learn to believe that what you perceive is "most likely true."

Then, *Live as if it is.*

Rainbow Light Shield

This is a powerful exercise from the Divine Mind for setting an exceptionally protective energy field around you. Once you have learned this technique, you need only *imagine* the shield for it to be there.

The pituitary gland is the *third eye.* Fixed at the base of the brain, this gland is the most important. The seventh chakra (energy center) in the body, this gland transmits telepathic and clairvoyant experiences. A Rainbow Light Shield is an *extra-strength prescription* for those few people who attract unwanted contact or negative influence from astral entities or people.

Begin this exercise with aura cleansing and deep breathing. Then develop a clear image in your mind of a shield of light that you can call to mind whenever you need protection.

Cleanse your aura.

- Sit in a comfortable position and begin deep breathing ... until you are deeply relaxed. Deep breathe and relax.

Clear your chakras.

- Allow your consciousness to *float,* and your mind to move toward creating protection.

- *Visualize your third eye* (at your forehead, between your eyes) as if it is projecting a ray from your brain outward. See the power of this *eye* moving forward through your brain, like a powerful ray of light, to the center of your forehead.

- *Now, imagine* that this *eye* is all-seeing and can be opened and closed at will. Practice now, through visualization, opening and closing your third eye. When it is closed, it is closed to *all* psychic input. When it is open, you are receptive to all psychic and *supra*-conscious perceptions and insights.

- *Now, imagine* a shield of brilliant blue light covering your third eye. This shield functions like a door that may be opened or closed by an electronic beam that only you control. Visualize this door as brilliant blue and totally impenetrable to all negative forces. This *blue door,* which only you can open or close (by your will) is a force field. It protects your third eye (your center of higher awareness) from all forces that are negative or harmful.

- *Now, visualize* this impenetrable *blue door* as pulled down and covering your third eye. See the blue door emitting a brilliant blue light. See the force field of this blue light radiating outward. See all negative forces *bouncing off* the blue light, unable to penetrate it. See these negative forces bounce off the blue light and dissipate into nothingness.

- *Now, extend* this impenetrable shield of brilliant blue light until it entirely surrounds your mind like a globe. You feel comfortable and you are still able to function normally, except you are more at peace and you are free of negative bombardments of *all* kinds—intentional and unintentional.

- *Now, extend* this impenetrable shield of brilliant blue light until it entirely surrounds your whole body and your whole aura. See this blue light as an impenetrable bubble that surrounds your bubble of white light.

- *Now see these lights* surrounded by a *rainbow light,* a rainbow light shield of all-color for total protection. These lights combined are a power of positive force.

- *Now, see* this impenetrable *shield of rainbow light* totally around your third eye, your mind, your whole body and aura.

- Say the word LIGHT and you are immediately relaxed.

- Say the word LIGHT and you are immediately at ease and protected within the force field of this brilliant rainbow light.

> *Guardian angels and protectors,*
> *watch over me throughout this day.*

> *I am safe and at peace.*

Keep this shield of rainbow light around you *at all times,* day and night, waking and sleeping. Be sure to put up this shield of light when you go to sleep and ask your guardian angels and protectors to watch over you.

Rainbow light is pure white light. White light is all colors combined. You may visualize either the rainbow light around you, or pure white light, or both—whatever works best for you and is the clearest visually in your mind, because the image you set in your mind makes the shield and protection real.

The most effective tool for protection is being centered through balancing your chakras. *Then* place the shields of light around your whole being, and ask your angels, soul, and Archangel Michael, to help you and protect you. They will.

Protection Affirmation 1

This is a follow-up technique for shielding yourself at will from all negative energies: a conditioned-response statement. The self-conditioning response word is LIGHT.

For full effect, be sure you already: Cleared your aura. Did the White Light Technique and/or Rainbow Light Shield.

You are deep breathing into deep relaxation. Count backward until you feel yourself drifting into a very deep level of consciousness and you feel loose and limp.

> *Every time I think or say the word LIGHT, I become relaxed and at ease.*

> *A shield of LIGHT surrounds me.*

> *Negative thoughts and feelings of others deflect off me.*

Whenever you say the word LIGHT or think the word LIGHT, or the word LIGHT pops into your mind, the shield of protection automatically projects around you.

You may add commands to protect your loved ones (family, friends, pets, home, car).[6]

---

6   Another good exercise for protection and shielding against negative forces is the Spiritual Protection Technique in Dick Sutphen's book *Past Lives, Future Loves.*

Protection Affirmation 2

This affirmation is most beneficial when you are relaxing, although you may repeat it and visualize it at any time, as often as you feel the need.

For the fullest effect, first cleanse your aura and take several long deep breaths.

Then visualize the bubble of white light *and* rainbow light shield around your whole body and aura.

To quickly induce relaxation, count backward from 20 while deep breathing.

Feel yourself drifting into deep relaxation ... until you begin to feel limp. (Count backward only until you begin to feel *deeply* relaxed.)

The negative thoughts and feelings of others do not harm me in any way.

An impenetrable shield of brilliant rainbow lights surrounds my body and mind.

I say the word LIGHT and I am relaxed, at ease, and protected within the force field of this brilliant rainbow LIGHT.

Protection also can be created by working with the elements of nature. Water, fire, and earth relieve and discharge negative energy. Flowers (and plants) are also effective for absorbing negative energy.7

---

7 Be sure to ask permission of the plants to be used in this way, honoring the life form.

VISUALIZATION MEDITATIONS
FOR
SELF-EMPOWERMENT

Visualization 1

Accepting

- Pause in stillness. Release ... breathing out regret, fear, sorrow, animosity.

- See your mind blank. See a movie theater screen in your mind. On the screen, in the distance, see a light. See the light coming toward you slowly. Closer and closer.

- In the light, see a picture. You are in the picture. You are resolving a concern in the picture.

- Take a moment to reflect.

- Listen for an insight within you.

- Trust the insight. Accept it.

- Now let go.

Visualization 2

Forgiving Yourself and Others

For peace within

The ability to forgive ourselves and others is an effective tool for being centered. Being centered helps us to be clear emotionally and mentally, feeling free of doubt and ambivalence, and to have *knowing* about our choices in life.

Forgiving Others - for your own peace within

Cleanse your aura, then deep breathe and relax. See around you a bubble of white light. Then visualize in your mind's eye the blank movie theater screen. You are going to act out four scenes of different types of forgiveness. Look upon the screen now.

- See a situation in which *you* have hurt someone else and you want forgiveness. Approach the person in the picture on the screen. See yourself asking him or her for forgiveness. See the person accepting your apology. See the two of you embracing in friendship.

  Now let it go. Let it fade.

- See an incident in which *someone else* has hurt you and you now wish to forgive that person. See him or her approaching you. See yourself offering forgiveness. See the person accepting your forgiveness. See the two of you embracing in friendship.

  Now let it go. Let it fade.

- See a situation in which you feel *you were right and innocent* and someone hurt or harmed you, causing you to feel bitter, angry, or resentful. Approach that person now. Offer him or her forgiveness. See that person accepting your forgiveness. See the two of you embracing in friendship.

Now let it go. Let it fade.

- See *an event for which you feel you can never forgive yourself.* See two images of yourself on the screen. See one of these images of yourself offering forgiveness to the second image of yourself. See the second image accepting forgiveness from the first image. See your two selves embracing in friendship. See these two images of yourself blending into one person. You feel happy and peaceful.

Keep this with you.

Forgiving Yourself - for peace within

Now to forgive yourself and all who have hurt you, begin deeply breathing and deeply relaxing.

Visualize a bubble of white light radiating outward from your center and completely surrounding you.

Now, see in your mind's eye a blank movie screen. One at a time, slowly, view and experience the following scenes:

A situation in which *you hurt someone* and you wish to be forgiven.

- See yourself approaching *(name)* in your mental picture on the screen.

- See yourself asking *(name)* for forgiveness.

- See *(name)* accepting your apology.

- See both of you embracing in friendship.

An incident in which *someone else hurt you* and you now wish to forgive *(name)*.

- *See (name)* approaching you.
- See yourself sincerely offering forgiveness.
- See *(name)* accepting your forgiveness.
- See both of you embracing in friendship.

A situation in which you feel *you were right and innocent* and someone hurt or harmed you, causing you to feel bitter, angry, or resentful.

- See yourself approaching *(name)* in your mental picture.
- See yourself sincerely offering *(name)* forgiveness.
- See (*name)* accepting your forgiveness.
- See both of you embracing in friendship.

An event for which *you feel you can never forgive yourself.*

- See two images of yourself on your mental screen.
- See one of your selves offer forgiveness to the other.
- See the other self accepting forgiveness from the first self.
- See both parts of you embrace in friendship.
- Now see these two images of yourself blending into one person.
- Feel happy and at peace.

Visualization 3

Communing with Your Soul and Angels

Higher Conscious Meditation

In a Higher Conscious Meditation, we can receive guidance from our Higher Conscious Self (oversoul, soul). We also may receive messages and insights from angels or Ascended Teachers or Masters.

- At the moment when you feel so moved, cleanse your aura.

- Then energize your chakra centers, guided by your body's natural movement with the flow of the vibration through your palms. Visualize the enhancement of the vibrations of your body.

- Attune by balancing your positive and negative polarities so there will be a continuous cycling of vibration from the cosmos through your body and back out again. Flow with humming, chanting, affirmations, prayers, whatever impresses you, until you reach a high state of rapport.

- As you do this Higher Conscious Meditation, flow with what comes to you. You may wish to use a recorder to free your mind and flow with channeling. Allow yourself to flow. Releasing emotions at the higher conscious level releases you from burdens. The answers you receive in *this* released state are true ones.

- Once you have reached your center—the point of strength and peace within—you will *know* who you are, what you are, and why. As you come back to your conscious self—you may again slip into doubt, but you will *know* your truth because you will have felt it. This experience of your truth will give you the stability and courage to pursue your dreams with certainty.

Visualize **white light** coming into your body through the top of your head.

- See the white light flowing into you, then spreading outward from your center—out, over, and around you.

- See yourself filled with the white light, bathed in the white light. In the white light, see yourself as bright as sunshine. You are vibrant energy, pulsing and alive. You are light, perfect and whole.

- Be at peace.

- Inwardly sense and perceive information from a high entity present. Be still. *Feel.* Allow a being of high spiritual vibration to be present. Be aware of a sensation or pressure, a touch or feeling, tactile in some manner.

- Now, release the feeling and let go. Take a long deep breath and release.

In your inner vision, imagine a **blank movie screen**.

- Visualize the screen as totally black. Then gray. Then light gray. Then dull white. Then pure white.

- Watch a shape come forward as a picture onto the pure white screen. The shape may have color, patterns, features. Allow yourself to *see* the shape. See the shape on the white screen. Look at the shape in close detail. Enlarge the picture. Zoom in for a closer look. Describe to yourself what you see.

- Now, release. Take a long deep breath and release.

*Now, be aware of a **fragrance.***

- You may ***smell*** this physically or sense it. Be aware of a scent that stands out as quite remarkable, as unique. Allow this scent to come to you from the vibration of the being who is present. Describe the fragrance to yourself. Identify it with the previous feeling and image.

- Now, release. Take a long deep breath and release.

*Now, be aware of a **taste.***

- This tactile texture or flavor is coming through your sense perceptions from the being present. The taste is unique. Identify the taste with the previous fragrance. Identify the taste and fragrance with the previous feeling. Identify the taste, fragrance, and feeling with the inner vision.

- All right now, release. Take a long deep breath and release.

Now, a thought comes into your mind.

- Listen to the words and repeat them to yourself.

- Then another thought. This thought is the ***name*** of the being or a word that identifies him or her. You clearly hear in your inner sanctum the telepathed word or name of the being. Listen, and repeat the word or name to yourself.

- Now mentally ask a ***question*** of the being. Pause. Listen for the telepathed answer that comes in response.

- Now ask, "Are you my Master Teacher?" Listen for the answer. Say, "If you are not my Master Teacher, who are you? What is your relationship to me?" Listen carefully to the thought that comes *into* your mind.

- Now, ask a question of your greatest concern. Listen for a brief answer or message.

- You have heard an answer.

- Now release, let go, relax, and be at peace. With a long deep breath, relax and let go.

Visualization 4

Self-Empowerment

The breath is the power.

This physical-mental-emotional-spiritual *rebalancing* works by oxygenizing.

Breathe deeply and continuously throughout the following exercise, through *both* nostrils simultaneously, with your mouth closed and breathing in and out so that you can *hear* the breath. (You may exhale through the mouth, or inhale and exhale through one nostril at a time.)

Allow the breath to be deeply penetrating, deeply focused, in through your crown, out through your toes, so that you feel light and tingly all over, especially tingling in the head. Breathe steadily. Your breath may be somewhat rapid, which is fine as long as it is in rhythm and you feel in harmony.

You may wish to hold a quartz crystal in each hand or one over your heart while doing the following affirmation-meditation. You may also wish to place several crystals in a circle around you, pointing inward. Quartz crystals can enhance and magnify your energy and presence.

You may wish to place your hands or fingers over your heart. Allow finger and hand movements/connections; fingertips touching, fingers folding/interlocking over your heart. This opens the heart chakra. Let these movements and placements be natural and instinctive. Do only what feels natural.

Follow your body. Follow your thoughts. If your inner thoughts change from this script, or continue beyond this script, follow and allow your own personal inner experience.

For chronic conditions and for initial practice, *allow one to one-and-a-half hours* for this *healing meditation.* By the third or fourth day of doing this meditation, you may begin to feel more natural and need less time, three-fourths to one hour.

When you complete the affirmation, rise slowly (in case you are temporarily light-headed).

Repeat each line of the following affirmation as often as you need to, until you feel *at-one,* resonant—until you feel inner healing, inner peace. Do each affirmation line in rhythm with breathing. Repeat each line until your body shakes or trembles with the energy, or shivers or involuntarily twitches. This can be subtle or slight. You may get very hot as your energy increases.

Affirm as if you mean it. If you don't resonate with the words used here, listen in your mind—or feel—and affirm *that.* But try this to start.

You may *pause to read each affirmation line* and still receive benefit as long as you (1) deep breathe and (2) continue until you shiver or overflow with the energy. Listen to your own rhythm.

Release may come in tears, when the heart is full. Allow the tears.

> *I am filled with the Father-Mother-I AM.*
> *I am a being of light.*
> *I resonate with the all mighty I AM.*
> *All that I am manifests fully out from me*
> *... and back to me again.*
>
> *All that I am is holy and divine.*
> *I am whole and filled with peace.*
> *My Father-Mother-I AM, heal me.*
> *I am.*
>
> *All that I am, I am now.*
> *The work that I do is healing.*
> *I heal. I give. I am.*
> *All that I do is Spirit in me.*
>
> *My Father-Mother-I AM,*
> *thank you, thank you.*

And so it is
this day
and every day.

For a most powerful personal healing and connection with the Divine, visualize a shaft of vibrant white light upward from the earth, up from your toes, resonating one at a time through each of your chakras.

- At each chakra, visualize its energy opening and expanding until you feel released (tingling, shivering, twitching—subtle or slight).

- Your breathing now may become more normal, steady and less intense. Focus on deepening your concentration. Just allow the breath to guide you into your own inner silence.

- Raise the stream of light upward to the next chakra (base, below belly button, below ribs, heart, throat, forehead, top of head, just above head to 8, 9, 10, 11, 12). At each chakra, the energy *pulses* until it releases and moves on to the next.

- Feel an alignment-shift straight up through your being into the Divine, as if a golden string has pulled you straight up.

- Open your heart and being to the guidance, wisdom and counsel of Higher Self.

I open myself to Ascended Masters, Teachers,
guides, guardians, angels, and protectors.

I am light. I am love. I am divinity.
I am that I am.

I am in the light and only the light.
My work is in the light and only the light.

My commitment is to the light.

*The golden ray of love, light, and protection
fulfills me and surrounds me.
I AM.*

I am love may be a soft affirmation that gently takes you deeper and deeper into the silence. Repeat until the wellspring of divine love overflows through your being.

I am love. I am light.

Now allow yourself to go deeply into a personal meditation. For this entire process, initially one-and-a-half to two hours. By the third or fourth day, one to one-and-a-half hours. Eventually total time about one hour on average. This is a powerful way to pray, affirm, and let go.

Allow yourself to experience whatever is flowing into your heart or being at this time. Allow yourself to affirm deeply whatever commitments, certainties, revelations, or realizations surface now in your mind from your whole self. The deeper you go, the more you will feel your body sink and let go.

For deepest concentration, focus your attention at your third eye. Continue gentle rhythmic breathing to commune. Complete with:

*I am that I am.
And so it is.*

BRAINWAVE AND HEART INTEGRATION

DEEP VISUALIZATION MEDITATIONS

from the Infinite Consciousness

These advanced techniques are from my book *Global Society 2.0,* received through my oversoul consciousness in 1985 and first published here (now in production, in "*The New Humanity*" Series).

Each of these *five* exercises is best practiced regularly, although not all on the same day. You may wish to alternate days. Perhaps a different exercise each day. At least three exercises is recommended, by the Divine Mind, per week for generating sufficient *breath* to transmute your physical and emotional bodies and, with that, the mental and spiritual bodies.

Read each exercise *slowly* while in deep relaxation. This will convey a calming and subduing energy.

Brain-Heart Visualization 1

Toning the Cellular Structure of Your Psyche and Body

Find a quiet place to reflect without interruption. Sit with your spine straight, feet flat on the floor and parallel, palms facing upward in your lap. (While learning these exercises, you may slightly shut your eyes so that you can read the directions while doing the exercises. After you have memorized the exercises, close your eyes when repeating them.)

Chakras	*Where in the Body*
Crown	soft spot top of head
Third eye	center of forehead
Throat	soft indentation
Heart	center of chest
Solar plexus	beneath ribs
Spleen	polarity, just below navel
Root	base of spine

Breathe in purple light through your crown chakra at the top of your head.

- *Feel* this purple light, its depth of tone and sparkling energy. Let the *purple* light spread outward from your crown and slowly flow downward through your body and chakra energy centers.

- *Release.* Focus the *purple* light down through your body from the top of your head. *Wash* the light slowly through *every* cell of your body.

Now a rich, vibrant emerald green. In the same way, go through all the chakras and through every cell of your body with the emerald green light.

Now snowy white. Beginning at the top of your head, feel a rich, soft white glistening down through all your chakras and through every cell of your body.

- Breathe deeply and very slowly *inhale,* from the tips of your toes all the way up above the top of your head. *Hold* for a moment. Then *exhale* slowly back down and through your body, all the way back down through the tips of your toes.

- *Inhale* through the exterior of your body and *release* breath through the interior of your body, flushing out all imbalances of the physical and emotional bodies.

Now lavender. Inhale the color lavender through the exterior of your body, and wash lavender down through your body, healing and clearing. Repeat. Repeat.

Now aqua. Inhale and release the color aqua. Repeat. Repeat.

Now white. Inhale and release the *gentle* healing color of white. Repeat. Repeat. Now let the imaging go.

These colors of the purifying force heal and transmute consciousness at all levels. The practice of visualization with color and tone, any way it is used, heals, resets and transmutes. The Divine Mind chose basic colors that have to do with this process. You may experiment with other combinations also, using three colors at a time on different days.

The *deep rich* colors set up a tone for healing, and reconstruct the cellular body to transform. The *soft gentle* colors are then able to pass through and cleanse every aspect of the cellular structure, including thought forms, and release all debris of the psyche and the bodies.

Brain-Heart Visualization 2

Transmuting to a Light Body

Less dense molecularly than a third-dimension physical body

Breathe in slowly to your center from all around you. Breathe in slowly the energy breath of the life force.

- When you release the energy breath, allow the life force to radiate outward in all directions throughout every cell of your body.

- As the life force passes through the walls of your body, it is transmuting the cellular structure of your form and lightening the density of your body.

- Breathe in - Absorb - Redigest - Transmute.

When you release and breathe out, as the transmuted energy radiates outward, it is transmuting the cellular structure of your body. Continue this rhythmic pattern, imagining (imaging) the light in the seven colors of the *rainbow,* starting with the darkest and going to the lightest.

From the bottom to the top, do the scale of: Red - Orange - Yellow - Green - Blue - Indigo - Violet.

On the out breath of the last color (violet), *release.*

Now breathe in golden light.

- Breathe in golden light and contain it in the center of your body (solar plexus below the ribs) while circulating the golden light *clockwise.* As you deep breathe, continue the circular movement of the golden light within your center.

- After a few moments, allow the golden light to radiate outward in a circular pattern into every cell of your body.

- After a few more moments, pause and move the golden light **counterclockwise** in the opposite direction. Then radiate the golden light outward in the circular pattern throughout every cell of your body.

- Radiate the golden light in through your head—from the top of your head, through the tips of your fingers, beyond the tips of your toes.

- You may experience this **radiating circle** of *golden light* around your extended fingers and toes reaching out, so that the light is actually a complete circle encompassing your body. The golden light radiates outward and transmutes your physical and emotional bodies.

- All right, briefly bring back the golden light to a **clockwise** circular movement. Hold the light *still* for a moment in your center. It is vibrating in a circle but more *still*. The focus on the golden light is in the center of your body. Bring the golden light to a *stillpoint*, even though it is still vibrating.

- Now send the golden light in *streams* from your center outward throughout your body, so the light is flowing outward in all directions, through every element of your body including your head.

- The golden light is now streaming from your center outward in a flowing motion, radiating outward continuously as rivers of golden light. Only the center of the light is moving, in a very gentle circular vibrating pattern.

- Now release. Breathe in more deeply and slowly.

- Continue breathing more deeply. Allow the golden light to be in you—radiating *as a sun* throughout your body.

- Now visualize this *sun* radiating from your center—your natural energy focus. Focus the light of this *sun* within you as a healing and transmuting energy.

- As this *sun* radiates outward, it is clearing, healing and transmuting the physical cellular structure of your body and, with that, your emotional body.

Now see the color of the light change to blue.

- See a clear blue light radiating outward, soothing and healing all aspects of your being—physical and emotional, mental and spiritual.

- Allow the clear blue color to gently *fade* as it continues to radiate through you. Know that this clear blue is transmuting and healing you.

- As the clear blue of this light *fades* from your inner vision, know that it is still with you and present. You are still focusing on the clear blue light, but less intently.

- No longer visualize the clear blue light. Simply know it is there. Simply feel its presence. Just allow it to heal, soothe, and release you.

- As you continue breathing deeply, allow yourself to let go into the rhythm of the radiating clear blue light from your center.

- As you breathe, bring the life force into your center and release it outward. The life force is continuously flowing into you, transmuting, and flowing outward. You are transmuting your physical body as well as all of your bodies, emotional, mental, and spiritual.

- *Hold this focus for five minutes*—while you move around and become involved in daily activities.

- Continue the breathing rhythm of this radiating life breath in and through the center of your being.

Brain-Heart Visualization 3

Healing Friendships

This is to release all expectations of friendships, to heal and forgive all disturbed energies within yourself and with others.

- Breathe in light and fill your body with light's vibrant source of comfort. Just breathe in light and feel light in every aspect of your being.

- Breathe in a light of *love* and *gentle discernment,* gentle *freedom* of feeling.

- Breathe in *calmness.*

- Breathe in *release* and *acceptance.*

- Breathe in a slow, gentle, rhythmic pattern of inhaling and releasing, a slow even rhythmic pattern of breath now. Slowly inhale. Focus, then release. Continue this rhythm.

As you breathe in, the light radiates gently and softly throughout your being.

As you release, the light releases outward and dissipates, clearing and cleansing as you let go.

- Breathe in *allowing.*

- Breathe in *gentleness.*

- Breathe in *acceptance.*

- Breathe in *forgiveness* ... and release. Do not tie forgiveness to any thoughts or images. Just *breathe in* forgiveness. *Feel* forgiveness and release.

- Breathe in *stillness.*

- Breathe in *allowing.*

- Breathe in *acceptance.*

- Breathe in *release.*

Now your breath becomes more *still* and more deep, longer and even. Your breath reaches more deeply, more relaxed now.

- Breathe in *perception.* ... now let go.

- Breathe in *friendship.* ... now let go.

- Breathe in *wisdom.*   ... now let go.

- Breathe in *forgiveness.* ... now let go.

- Breathe in *willingness.* ... now let go.

- Breathe in *understanding.* ... now let go.

- Breathe in *being.*   ... release slowly.

- Breathe in *acceptance.* ... slowly let go.

- Breathe in *hope.*
  ... feel hope through your being as you release.

- Breathe in *gentleness.*
  ... feel gentleness transmute you to an even deeper level as you release.

Go deeper and deeper now into your being.

- Breathe in *love* ... then breathe out love. Radiate love outward around you.

- Breathe in *love.* Feel love transform your energy, your feelings. Allow love to radiate outward as you release love. Breathe in love, healing your being.

- The healing energy of *love* releases outward from you and through you and continues to radiate outward around you.

- Breathe in *love.* The energy radiates in you and through you and outward through every aspect of your reality.

- Breathe in *love,* healing and transmuting your being and releasing love outward to every person and everything around you, continuously and forever.

- Breathe in *love* and allow love to flow through you and outward to all around you.

- Breathe in **acceptance.** Allow acceptance to flow outward to all around you, endlessly and forever. Breathe in acceptance ... and release acceptance to all around you.

- Breathe in *love* ... and release love to all around you.

- Breathe in *being* ... and release being to all around you. Breathe in and allow being. Just be in the breath. Just be the breath.

- Breath is *All That Is.* Breath is all that is. Receive breath and give breath back. Just let the breath go.

- Let the breath go.

Brain-Heart Visualization 4

Healing the Traumas and Conditions of Your Life

Dissipating Barriers and Integrating Your Etheric Body

There is a physical force called ether. This force is substance and may be utilized in physical reality in many ways. We may use ether (etheric matter) for vitality, which is the breath, or prana.

Etheric force is energy. It may be tapped or utilized. Therefore, let us focus on synchronizing your physical form with your etheric body, bringing these into alignment so that you feel more complete and more whole.

The disciplines we practice are a part of this bonding, and seeking communication with others is a form of bonding. Bonding means to unify, to a whole, the many parts that we are. We are not only a physical form. We are also an etheric body, many other bodies as well. The focus here on the etheric body is to give us substantial information for working with it daily.

"The results will bear immediate fruit," says the Divine Mind, who channeled this meditation to a group during a workshop, "not only in emotional balance, but in the manifestation of an ideal—upon which to focus your attitude."

The beginning of full integration and becoming a whole self is to look at our **attitudes**.

First, a brief attunement exercise:

- See a clear blue light within your center, pulsating with your rhythm—a *living force.*

- *As you inhale:* See the clear blue light absorbing into the bloodstream of your body, into the cells of your flesh, and purifying your physical body.

- *As you exhale:* See all excretions of imbalance and impurity of the physical body dissipating. Attuned to the center of your being, see yourself releasing all blocks—emotional and physical.

- Now allow a thought to come to mind, an area of focus meaningful in your life, a condition or a relationship. Allow an image (or a thought form) to come to mind. Notice your emotional feelings. Identify and name these various feelings you are experiencing related to this subject.

- Now sense your body. Notice any sensations, trembling, vibration, withdrawal or impact, any kinks or soreness. Now breathe out and release.

The challenge in any degree of reality is in *letting go,* learning to flow rather than need to control. Since that is a state of mind and has nothing to do with the physical form, letting go is a permanent process that is real. Being able to dissipate any wrong toward you or your limiting attitudes is something that will prove useful to you today, tomorrow, and forever.

Now imagine your physical form.

- See your body's outline and see its substance.

- Become aware of the energy presence of the **attitude** and **thought** you have about your subject. See that attitude as a presence or energy force and observe how it impacts your physical body.

- In your mind's eye, as you look at both your form and the energy force of the idea, look at how they work together, how one impacts the other; whether the connection is smooth, natural and dissipated, or whether there are conflicts. Simply be aware of these.

- Breathe in the clear blue light, breathe out all stress, and release.

Now become aware of **another** body.

- See superimposed through you and around you a greater body It looks very similar to your physical body, except it is not as dense and it is more magnetic. There is more free-flow of the vital force through it.

- Notice the light and color of the dense physical body. Then notice the light and color of this less dense, lighter etheric body. Feel the difference. Observe the difference.

Now look upon the energy force of the **idea** of your subject.

- Look at that energy force as a color and a light. Observe the way in which the subject-idea impacts the physical body. Observe the impact of the color and light, and notice the mixture.

- At the same time, become aware that the subject-idea is impacting the etheric body. Notice the effect of that energy force on the etheric body. Notice the light and color, any energy patterns, any movement patterns.

- Breathe in the clear blue light, and release.

Now become aware of the energy force of your subject-idea.

- Imagine that you are standing beside a cool stream. Feel the freshness of nature, the free creative power, and the release of it upon your being.

- Look into the water, which is very clear, and see your reflection. Notice how you perceive yourself as you look at your reflection. Notice how you experience who are you are: the image.

- Dip your hands into the pool, bring up the fresh water and drink it. Think of it as pure substance, pure vital force, which you now take into your being to resupply and nurture your physical body, etheric body, and emotional body.

- As you drink of that *vital force* and feel it radiating through you—synthesizing your various bodies—it is as if one body is overlapping the other. As you drink in the vital force of life, these bodies meld, they become one, simply extending *endlessly,* without any real distinction or separateness.

- As you begin to feel more centered and *realigned* with your natural powers, the attitudes and emotions connected with your subject-area are healed through this same change of energy in your body.

- As the bodies become one—merged (simply a blend from the inner to the outer, a blend from the physical through all the bodies, extensions of the same light)—the energy force of your subject-idea is affected in the same manner. Whatever is not in alignment with that blend is dissipated through it, caught up in it and changed along with it, redigested, and synergized.

- So now, place the subject-idea before you and look upon it again to observe it more objectively. You see the person or the face of the one who is involved in the situation with you, you begin to realize that attachments are dissolving. Needs and extremes are dissolving, and you are flowing as you look upon that face, that condition.

Now become aware of yourself - the blended whole being.

- Look out around you at the various disparaging conditions of your life, as if you are on a vast landscape and you are the one thing that is complete and blended—in the way the ocean blends from one color to the next but it is all one, in the way your breath blends with the air around you yet it is all one.

- Look upon the conditions around you in your life that do not seem to have the same balance of energy. As you interact with them in this imagery, you are aware of the separation between you and your subject-idea. You might see that separation as a wall, a wall in the sense that you do not understand the subject and do not know how to link *with* it.

- You are now aware of your *blended whole being*—the physical, etheric, and all other bodies (emotional, mental, spiritual). You know you *are* the vital force, that you not only drink it in from life but also give it out, in the same way as a flower.

- Give it out now. Give out your vital force. Send it and *wave* it outward through all those conditions that surround you.

- Focus in on one condition in particular. Allow the vital force to move from your being through that subject, condition, relationship. Watch the barriers disintegrate between you and complete integration with your subject-idea. The walls disintegrate between you and the idea, desire, condition ... until you realize it is simply an extension of you and is no longer foreign.

- When your subject-idea begins to have the same energy flow and balance *as* you, it is as if your body has simply *extended* that much in that direction. The subject-idea is nothing different or separate from you.

Do this now in circumference, in all directions outward.

- Simply imagine all disparaging relationships and conditions in your life as *energy forces* that surround you. Vibrate out the blend of *oneness* with yourself. Vibrate it outward until you begin to see it transform all those energy forces surrounding you, until all are complete and you are greater and larger than you were before.

- Everything dissipates now that is not a part of *the blend* ... until there is nothing left but simply *extensions* of your bodies, extensions of your being, and they are a part of *that* reality.

- Being aware of this, bring it all back to the present. Think about who you are *in this moment.* Think about what difference it makes in your feelings toward yourself. Think about what difference it makes in your attitude toward life around you. *Feel* what it is like to be open and simply extending the blend of who you are through everything that is called life. *Feel* what it is like to be open.

• All right now, relax and let go. We are done.

The etheric body is a *power pack* for our human beingness. It is in the etheric body that things first manifest before coming into physical reality. It is in the etheric body that thoughts form, ideas congeal, and conditions are first encountered.

When we are so attuned that we can introspectively observe our own etheric body, we can then discern when something in our life is not in alignment and not bearing the results we desire. We can alter the magnetic properties of that condition in its *etheric state* by focusing our mind and thought process to our etheric form.

Be aware of altering the magnetic properties of the ether, even though subjectively. Be aware of creating matter by first *feeling-sensing-perceiving-defining* the etheric matter. This is an introspective process that may or may not include intuitive/psychic perceptions.

Once we realize that thought is energy, we can then understand its direct effect on ether (etheric matter). Therefore, we can make substantial changes in both our body and the things we manifest: by working first at the etheric level.

Rather than demand physical results, introspectively discern what is in balance or not ... in your etheric state. Look at the magnetic polarities. Set up the balance. *Then* bring it into physical manifestation ... as a result of your perception.

Go within now for a few more moments and consider what *your* etheric body is, how it feels, and how that is relevant now to you as a physical person ... and is the source of your pivotal force and spiritual presence in the world.

Brain-Heart Visualization 5

Heart Integration

Joy is an emotion that can be ferreted out of the psyche of consciousness. Joy feels its way into our experience.

We are not found responsible for much of the ineptness of our personality, says the Divine Mind. We are evolving our spirit.

We revolve around a core essence, which is divinity. Meditation is a practice that integrates this essence into our personality. Meditation attunes us to our divine potential.

Happiness comes when we are able to release our fears—by accepting this divine essence as our basic being. Our personality evolves as we recognize *allowing.*

Consciously *receiving breath* cleanses and heals the body. *Holding breath* focuses our being. *Releasing breath* cleanses and heals and sets up a reciprocal pattern that may then flow through us as easily as water in a stream.

The following meditation is a little bit different than the previous three. Become quiet. Breathe evenly and gently. Regard yourself gently, and imagine that the most wonderful experience of your life is taking place.

- Begin to breathe in deeply.

- Think of yourself as water. Blend. Be a river. Be quiet and calm as a river.

- Widen your banks of experience. Broaden your movement along the way. Reach out to the perimeters of your existence.

- Move naturally. Breathe. Breathe evenly and consciously. Release through breathe. Inhale ... hold ... exhale (8-4-8 count). Release.

Now, focus through breath.

- Feel yourself lift up in spirit. Light is energy. Energy fills you as you breathe in light.

- **Breathe in life.** Release the shadows of fear and expectation. Release to *divine intent.*

- Surround yourself with an imagined potential of your spiritual enlightenment. Immerse yourself in acceptance of the breath of joy.

- **Breathe in imagined potential** of your total essence in joy. Begin to realize that you *are* free of expectations. Allow yourself to evolve in the moment of this experience.

- Breathe in the essence of **calm.** Breathe in **stillness.** Flow to your own spirit as water flows, to and fro.

- Follow the natural inclination of your path. Allow it. Trust your path. Trust your imagination to follow your path. Trust your innocence and your discernment. Breathe in acceptance of yourself at all levels of devotion. Release confusion, irritation, and fear.

- **Breathe in light.** Breathe out friendship. Breathe in imagined potential ... and help yourself forgive.

- The key is the *rhythm* of breath ... deeply. The only effort is breathing *deeply.* The focus is breathing *deeply.*

- Restore blessedness. Bless yourself. Bless your life. Bless those who share life with you. Release them in the light.

- Become your desire. Forgive.

A true master of life releases and forgives in the music of being, in the rhythm of the breath.

Breathe deeply.

Be who you are

... in the breath.

This is total. This is complete. Everything comes from this. Understanding, peace, and wisdom come from the integrated breath. You are free.

Breathe.

Revealed Teachings

Appendices

The Secret to Manifestation

from the Infinite Consciousness

To support yourself adequately in the physical, think about how things are formed, how matter is created:

> First, it is *idea.*
> Then it is *thought.*
> Then it is *matter.*

Everything is a process and follows certain rules. Everything that is manifest is following a natural law—regardless of the speed with which it manifests or the manner in which it manifests.

First, look at your ideas, which are in part attitude and in part beliefs. An idea itself must be in harmony with your soul's desire for your life. So, look at what you are considering to manifest and whether that specifically is in alignment with your total need.

Idea is the beginning. Now be aware of that idea as *etheric force,* and imagine that it is born within you. Even if you don't fully comprehend your idea, you are creating whatever you comprehend. The more clear and cognizant you are in the idea, the more clearly it will manifest according to your desire.

*Imagine the idea within you as an **etheric force**, as a blue light.*

- Now expand your being: you the blended self, your bodies, the whole. Just being who you are, breathing and emitting *etheric force.*

- Energy (the prana) leaves your presence, in the way a flower breathes. Be aware that you are emitting a certain force by the whole concept you are, not only thoughts and beliefs. Feel your whole focus emitting a *force.*

*Imagine you—the whole—glowing and vibrating a **force**.*

- See whatever blocks are around you as little spots or shadows on your whole force.

- Continue emitting the force, vibrating it outward.

- Consciously dissipate the shadows. Dissipate them as a matter of course. Don't put all your attention on one little dark spot. Simply know you are releasing them.

Focus your whole being on vibrating outward this *energy force—* what you are—and that your unlimited supply of power has no restraints of any kind.

- Emit and vibrate outward the unlimited supply of your being (which is what life is).

- As a matter of course, whatever shadows happen to be in your personality, simply dissipate them as you *vibrate your force outward.*

The key is the way in which we look upon who we are. *We* are the substance of life itself.

There might be appropriate times to focus on something discordant in our attitude or personality. So, another constant approach is the way you see yourself. Whatever activities you participate in, stabilize, maintain, and motivate your real self — which is always clear.

Now imagine the idea of poverty around you.

- See this thought form as *fog.* Know that you are the life force of the universe. Accept that, be that, and vibrate that outward as sunshine, clearing away the fog.

- Remember that you are light and the light is always there. Focus on radiating your light outward to dissipate the fog around you. Thought forms that are unclear, clear them.

It is important to acknowledge the fog. Yet, it is more important to wholeheartedly identify with the sunshine, to *be* the light, to remember that light is your real Self—because everything is a result of where we place our focus.

In terms of results, remember: Everything begins as etheric force. Ideas must be cognizant to match our desire. Ideas must be in harmony with your own sense of who you are. If there is any discord in the match, the results will not be desirable.

These are basic laws of physics: What appears to be physical is actually a denser form of energy. What appears to be thought or mind is a different form of energy. What is created in one will manifest in the other. If the results are not what you desire, release that result, allow for it, dissipate it, and manifest a different focus.

Relationships

To deal with different levels of emotion in *relationships* and with feeling separate, first identify your own synergy, feel yourself blended (the different parts of self). Feel it all blended as simply extensions of you.

From the blended Self, be aware of different persons and your relationships with them. Be aware of what appears to be separation and different feelings or perceptions.

Now radiate outward your sunshine.

- Allow that warmth to melt your self-imposed barriers and fears.

- As the rays of your sunshine reach outward in all directions, the warmth dissipates the differences, the separateness, and you begin to identify your experience of that person as really an extension of your *blend,* an extension of your vital force.

• Radiate your warmth outward.

There are more subtle bodies than the physical and etheric, but these are the most significant in terms of physical reality.

Remember, everything that is, is preceded by a different level of dimension. Before something becomes physical, it is first in etheric force, including the physical body. Even ideas and feelings are first formulated in the etheric self, which can be cleansed and healed, then reapplied in the physical.

Regarding relationships, it is one thing to look at our perceptions and ideas about a person. It is more important to understand that our experience of a relationship is an extension of our own being and we either blend or non-blend with that person.

• *Focus on radiating warmth, the sunshine of your being.* When you look at the person, be aware whether you feel a separation between you.

• *Now radiate the warmth of your being.* Release yourself to the warmth and allow the warmth to penetrate the relationship.

• See all barriers *dissolve.*

The key is where you place your focus. So, focus not on differences. Focus on being a whole Self, radiating outward your warmth. This transforms the conditions around you.

Be not afraid of your power. Be not afraid to accept yourself as a balanced, content and happy individual, who is on the Earth to share.

The Source of All That Manifests

The etheric body is an energy force. It is a combination of the astral body, emotional body, and mental body. It is our power pack. This energy force is not distinct from the bodies; it is *how* the bodies work together.

Etheric force is a less dense form than the physical, but closely akin to it. The astral body is a part of the etheric force.

People who work with healing are primarily working with the etheric body. If the result is accepted in the recipient's psyche, healing manifests in the physical. If the result is not accepted, it won't manifest.

Everything that manifests begins in ether. It is first in the unseen, before it comes into manifestation. In the etheric is where work needs to be done to get more immediate results.

You can visualize the desired result, but be aligned with what you want and make sure it is something you really need.

In working with your soul, it is important to acknowledge who you are — a whole blended Self. Soul is your sunshine, all of your bodies, your blended personality. Soul is all the parts of who you are, all the levels, all the aspects.

To be one with your soul is to focus not on separation but on the whole:

Give out your light.

As you give out your light, so you receive what you desire.

Your warmth and openness open the way.

A Vision

March 5, 1982 during seven-planet alignment

A delicate fragrance of rose potpourri filled my quiet room. I curled beneath my periwinkle-blue afghan and gazed out the bay window at the prisms of afternoon snow filling the crisp Colorado air, floating down softly and blanketing the earth white. The resonant dancing lights reached into my soul and embraced me.

Alive. I am. Forever.

In that moment, I could see beyond all boundaries, through all, and familiar thoughts streamed into my mind:

Be still. Be still and know that God is in you. Be still.

This mantra into my mind soothed me, calmed me, stroked away my fears.

Be still. Be still and know that God is in you. Be still.

Drowsiness overcame me and I drifted into a light nap, wherein I saw an iridescent figure. The familiar light-being took my hand, and warmth flowed through me. We lifted beyond this world to a very bright hall and stood before a large double door. It opened and we entered a lovely garden of flowers, with singing birds and flowing fountains.

The light-being departed and a tall, ageless, spiritual master walked toward me. His stride implied an inner strength born from much experience. Yet he came without grandeur, with a clear and steady gentleness. His brown hair and beard complemented his modest, brown priest's robe with a hood, of the ancient archetypal order of Melchizedek.

This handsome man, looking to be in his forties, came to me like a father. He came to me as a friend. His deep, brown eyes revealed a quiet and mellow nature.

"My name is Samuel," he said.

He took my hand and we strolled through the garden, as he explained that in one lifetime he had been known as the prophet

Samuel in the biblical Old Testament. After many lifetimes and inner explorations, he had grown beyond the boundaries of external reality and the struggles of human life. No longer bound to a body, he had ascended as his true Self into the timeless realms as one of the Unseen, now neither masculine nor feminine.

That was when he remembered he was an oversoul—*my* oversoul, the being from whom I first came to exist as an independent personality.

Until age thirty, I had journeyed throughout my life without consciously knowing of my oversoul's existence. Yet Samuel had guided me. His feelings had impressed me; and his thoughts had reached into my deepest self, embodying the soul presence into my life.

Samuel and I now came to a room of mirrors. "Why have you come?" he asked me.

"I want to know," I answered humbly.

"What do you want to know?"

"Whatever you will show me."

We walked through the room, looking at my own many reflections of different incarnations, and Samuel said of other Ascended Masters, angels, and himself, "We have little more knowing than you, but we have come far since physical life. Perhaps our insights and understanding will help you and your friends find an easier way."

"What can I do?" I asked.

"Give. That is all we ask. Let others know that life is not coming to any end. Let them know that they are each a divine aspect of the universal life force. Let them know that beings exist who respect and love them and offer support on request. Let them know all that we will tell you. Be our messenger. Let us teach through you."

We returned to the garden and, as Samuel departed, a tall slender woman with long midnight-black hair approached me. She gazed at me warmly with love and affection, and a reverence fell over me. Alexandra was the other half of me, my "twin flame," who also originally had come from the same oversoul; then she and I had decided to explore different kinds of reality as separate selves.

"My gift," she said, "is to give you all you have known and to lift you up. Prepare yourself, my friend. Join me now."

We walked and I listened and learned, transcending into expanded visions and hope.

"Indeed," said Alexandra, "there is always hope."

She and I planned the rest of my current life and I came to remember what I had known before about the realms of limitless thought.

We then traversed the universes and I brought back memories of these sojourns, which I share in this and many other books.

"Embrace all, be all," said Alexandra. "Know that your dreams are already fulfilled, even as you give yourself to them."

More About the Author

Charol Messenger spontaneously awakened to the universal consciousness at two a.m. November 2, 1975. As a result of this mystical activation, she has the spiritual gifts of clearly hearing, discerning, and interpreting the language of the soul—the "language of light."

Charol is a translator of esoteric knowledge and the etheric Akashic Records into human language in practical, everyday terms. All of the phases of her spiritual development that followed the awakening came upon her unbidden consciously and without any preparation or training; nevertheless, each phase was a part of the greater Soul Plan for this incarnation.

Carrying the signature and blueprint of her oversoul—the biblical prophet Samuel—Charol "elected" to be born in July 1945, between VE Day and VJ Day at the end of World War II, to be part of the upcoming transformative social changes on planet Earth.

In the fall of 1975, Charol encountered a life-threatening situation over several weeks. During highly charged and shattering encounters with dark spirits, she faced the "dark night of the soul." Latent psychic abilities and spiritual sight flooded to the surface of her consciousness, saving her physical life and her sanity. Thrust into dire circumstances and bombarded in her mind by images and tauntings by demons, she turned to prayer for the first time in fifteen years and asked God for guidance and protection. With the wisdom and strength of an old soul, she stood against the forces of darkness, stubbornly standing in the light and refusing to give in.

At the culmination of this "long dark night of the soul," Charol saw and heard the chorus of angels in heaven, and their ethereal light illuminated her bedroom during an *overlighting* by her oversoul consciousness. The outcome of this ordeal was the beginning of merging that higher consciousness into the physical body, mind, and personality.

This "soul merge," known esoterically as the Third Initiation, took six-and-a-half years to fully integrate. From five days before, through five days after March 5, 1982 (the day of a seven-planet alignment), this oversoul integration completed spontaneously, evidenced by eleven days of continuous heightened awareness and euphoria during which the oversoul consciousness fully embodied.

Two months later, in May, Charol was wakened out of a deep sleep by a gentle inner voice speaking *into* her mind, the voice of an angel on her soul council. This was the beginning of a writing phase during which Charol received, through inner dictation, several books from the oversoul consciousness on the spiritual path, the history and origin of the angels and how they help humanity, and our evolving human society. Charol received these books one at a time, taking dictation from the clear inner voice between the hours of two and four a.m., when she was wakened out of a deep sleep each night by an inner prodding. As she heard each word or phrase, she repeated it into a tape recorder. For the next twelve years, Charol transcribed, light edited, and integrated the information at a deep level of the Self. She did not publish these works; she only shared portions of the early pages with workshop participants as handouts, and with close friends.[8]

Then in 1994 another spontaneous event occurred during a six-month 24/7 period of exalted consciousness that resulted from very deep and prolonged meditative states, two hours at a time, daily. Having left a full-time job in April, Charol spent 100 percent of her time committed to renewing the connection with her spiritual Self, and she thrived on the rejuvenation.

---

8   In addition to oversoul, senders of the 1982 portions of this book on how time and matter manifest in fourth-dimension physical reality were Alexandra and Josiah on Charol's soul council (described in *Wings of Light* and *You 2.0*). Alexandra also wrote the 1982 portions on mind and its functions regarding fourth-dimension consciousness and the fourth-dimension human body. Alexandra is part of Charol's same oversoul, from the same *original* spark of soul, and is currently a higher-dimensional being. Alexandra and Charol's first incarnation is relayed in *The Memory* (in revision). In addition to being the *muse* behind all of the Messenger books, Alexandra wrote *You 2.0* vol. I on Higher Self initiation and integration (workshop handout in 1987 was titled "The Daily Routine of a Developing Initiate"). (Other early pages handed out were "Higher Consciousness Workbook" the early development of the completed *Intuition for Every Day* and "Visions of Serendipity" the early draft of soon-to-be-published *Angels of Serendipity*.)

After seven weeks, during an especially deep meditation, Charol *lifted* to a place in higher consciousness she had never reached before (and didn't know she could, had not sought it nor expected it). Writing from this new pristine place within the soul—the most pure place one can reach and bring back the insights into the world— Charol wrote four new books within four months, and a fifth soon after. She spent all of her waking hours transcribing (and absorbing) the inner-dictated materials; which, interestingly, she now received in her own point of view as if she had sat down and written them, including the anecdotes about her own life, which she had never before consciously realized.

Into these five books from the Higher Mind, the same essential ideas and topics were conveyed as had been received twelve years previously, except now in new words and with flawless writing: the angels in our everyday lives *(Wings of Light* and *Walking with Angels)*, the spiritual path and our eternal soul journey *(The Soul Path)*, humanity's first incarnation *(The Memory)*, and the origins and evolution of humanity *(The New Humanity,* 1st Ed., which is Vol. I in the 2012 updated and expanded *Humanity 2.0;* the original *New Humanity* concept draft was received in 1982, then re-received spontaneously in 1994, as you see it).

The revelations, mystical knowledge, and prophecies in all of these books are written in the Higher Mind, through the oversoul consciousness. All of the books are published verbatim as received, word for word; except for light editing, renaming and rearranging some chapters, and adding subheadings.

As a futurist and global visionary, awakened to cosmic consciousness and her oversoul in 1975, then the I AM Consciousness in 1994, Charol is a *spiritual revealer,* attuned to the undercurrent hum sweeping through humanity today. She is revealing humanity's long foretold evolutionary transformation—that is happening *right now.*

Humanity is in *transcension.* We are in it, now.

Recommended
Movies, Books, Audio, Video

First, I highly recommend *Networked Intelligence (Vernetzte Intelligenz)* by von Grazyna Fosar and Franz Bludorf, published 2001 in German, www.fosar-bludorf.com.

The following excerpt opens the discussion on how science is identifying greater capacities of the brain, including what have been considered extraordinary abilities, such as clairvoyance and telepathy—which I believe are innate within all human beings and will be evidenced more and more as humanity's evolutionary leap continues:

"New research suggests that human DNA is a virtual biological Internet and superior in many aspects to the artificial one. Could the latest Russian scientific findings help to explain the phenomena such as clairvoyance, intuition, spontaneous and remote acts of healing, self-healing, affirmation techniques, unusual light, auras, spiritual masters, the mind's influence on weather patterns, and much more? The answer may be yes.... Only 10% of our DNA is being used for building proteins.... The other 90% has been called 'junk DNA.'"

I also highly recommend:

2017 movie, *A Dog's Purpose,* based on the book *A Dog's Way Home* by w. Bruce Cameron

2016 movie, Marvel's *Dr. Strange*

2017 book, *Gifts from the Edge,* Claudia Watts Edge, a personal favorite, true insights and visions of life beyond death

In addition:

Hands of Light, Barbara Ann Brennan

Vision, Ken Carey, Harper San Francisco

Mastery Through Accomplishment, Hazrat Inayat Khan

Freedom in Exile: The Autobiography of the Dalai Lama

Surfing the Himalayas, Frederick Lenz

The Seat of the Soul, Gary Zukav

Living with Joy, Sanaya Roman

The Possible Human, Jean Houston

The Cultural Creatives, Paul H. Ray

Initiation, Elizabeth Haich

The Sacred Journey: You and Your Higher Self, Lazaris

Space-Time and Beyond, Toben and Wolf

Illusions, Jonathan Livingston Seagull, Richard Bach

The Education of Oversoul Seven, Jane Roberts

Psychic Self-Defense and Well-Being, Melita Denning and Osborne Phillips

The Impersonal Life, DeVorss & Co., Publishers

Life and Teaching of the Masters of the Far East, Baird T. Spalding

The Celestine Prophecy, James Redfield, Warner Books

"Getting in the Gap," Wayne Dyer

Pathways to Mastership, audio set, Jonathan Parker; Gateways Institute

"Chakra Balancing and Energizing" audio, Dick Sutphen

Joseph Campbell videos on mythology

I have not read the following books, so as not to influence my own writings, but I recommend them based on their topics, for a broad view of what visionaries are sharing.

The Third Millennium, Ken Carey, Harper San Francisco

The Power of Now, The New Earth, Eckhart Tolle

Bashar: Blueprint for change, Darryl Anka, New Solutions Publishing

New Cells, New Bodies, New Life! Virginia Essene, S.E.E. Publishing

You Are Becoming a Galactic Human, Virginia Essene and Sheldon Nidle

www.ingramcontent.com/pod-product-compliance
Lightning Source LLC
Chambersburg PA
CBHW031954040426
42448CB00006B/357